The
American
Spirit

The
American
Spirit

Celebrating the Virtues and
Values That Make Us Great

Brian Tracy *and* Edwin J. Feulner, PhD

THOMAS NELSON
Since 1798

NASHVILLE   DALLAS   MEXICO CITY   RIO DE JANEIRO

Note: Historical American documents quotes without accompanying endnotes are found at the Cato Institute's website, www.Cato.org.

Published in Nashville, Tennessee, by Thomas Nelson. Thomas Nelson is a registered trademark of Thomas Nelson, Inc.

Thomas Nelson, Inc., titles may be purchased in bulk for educational, business, fund-raising, or sales promotional use. For information, please e-mail SpecialMarkets@ThomasNelson.com.

Library of Congress Cataloging-in-Publication Data

Tracy, Brian.
  The American spirit : celebrating the virtues and values that make us great / Brian Tracy and Edwin J. Feulner.
     p. cm.
  Includes bibliographical references and index.
  ISBN 978-1-59555-337-9
  1. National characteristics, American. I. Feulner, Edwin J. II. Title.
  E169.12.T69 2012
  973--dc23   2012006061

Printed in the United States of America

12 13 14 15 QG 6 5 4 3 2

To our families—first among society's little platoons and the fundamental unit upon which the American Spirit rests and is renewed.

From Ed to my wife, Linda, and to E. J., Wendy, Betsy, and Sara, and to Emily, Chris, and Wills.

From Brian to my wife Barbara, and to my wonderful children: Christina, Michael, David, and Catherine.

Contents

Introduction

My upbringing was midwestern conventional. Mom and Dad instilled the entrepreneurial spirit in me from an early age, and my political views were developed in an open and free atmosphere. A professor of history introduced me to Erik von Kuehnelt-Leddihn, who penned a minor classic, *Liberty or Equality*, and to Russell Kirk, who authored the magisterial volume *The Conservative Mind*. Political discussions were intense and eye-opening, but they were civil. I learned my friends and I could disagree with each other without being disagreeable—something that seems to be lacking in today's Washington and indeed in many academic settings.

Coming to Washington was like arriving in another world, and my political and philosophical views were put to hard tests. I was hooked—not on the politics of the place, but on the policy implementation of the governmental process. As a fellow at a then start-up think tank—later as a congressional staffer, a political aide to the secretary of defense, and the cofounder of what has become a major American institution—I relished the process of making laws, of giving real Americans, from Elmhurst and from La Jolla, a chance to experience the best of a free society.

My personal story underscores my frequent claim that "I am Washington's greatest optimist." Even today, I remain optimistic about our nation and our people.

In an earlier book, with Doug Wilson, I called our fellow citizens back to first principles—to examine every proposal from government in the light of its ability to offer further opportunities to each of us and to bring us together as a people.

In this book, my longtime friend and colleague Brian Tracy and I share our view of the real core of America, of American virtues and values, of those characteristics that we share and that are so noble and transforming both here and around the world.

We also share our view of things going on in America that we *don't* like, not simply because they raise the deficit or delay our economic recovery or promote unemployment, but because they threaten to change the character of the American people in some very far-reaching and fundamental ways.

In his farewell remarks to his ministers in 1955, Winston Churchill said, "Man is spirit." It is this spirit—this American Spirit—that Brian and I wish to preserve above all else. So long as it remains alive and kicking, we are confident that all the problems facing our nation will eventually sort themselves out satisfactorily. But should it ever be impaired or transformed, the brightest policy experts from the best think tanks won't be able to arrest our inevitable decline.

Whatever your views about marginal tax rates, the gold standard, debt-to-GDP ratios, the Laffer Curve, and similar policy issues, we hope you will come to share our belief that an American Spirit exists, that it defines us as a people, and that it deserves to be preserved.

Edwin Feulner

February 2012

When I was a young man, I set out on a journey of discovery that eventually took me to ninety countries on six continents. Having started with no money and no high school diploma, very early I began asking the question, *Why is it that some people are more successful than others?* This question saved my life.

As I grew and educated myself, I studied such philosophers as Socrates, Plato, and Aristotle, all of whom asked, *How shall we live together in order to be happy?* These early thinkers saw man as a social animal and gave careful consideration to the best way for society to be organized for the greatest good. This question led me into a lifelong quest to understand why some countries, and even parts of countries, are more successful than others the world over and throughout history.

By the time I was eighteen, I realized I did not want to live in a world where America, with its American ideals, was not the dominant power. The twin isms of socialism and communism were powerful influences in the world at that time, and they exerted an attraction on many people who should have known better. I concluded the American ideals of freedom, equality, individual rights, self-reliance, free enterprise, respect for private property, civil society, and the rule of law were the finest principles to which man has aspired in all human history.

Today, millions of Americans are not clear about why the United States is the greatest country on earth and in all human history. Overseas, large numbers of people disapprove of America and the American way. Our aim in writing this book is to explain clearly what it means to be an American and why each American can be proud of being a citizen of this great country. We also want to explain to the world why Americans are an exceptional people, the "almost chosen" people of Abraham Lincoln. Every person reading these pages will emerge with a better understanding of the burden and the glory that come with being an American.

In a speech not long ago, the writer Midge Decter, who had switched from being a New York leftist hypercritical of America to a solidly pro-American conservative, explained what had caused her conversion. "I looked," she said, "at the ideal upon which America was founded, and to which I am committed, and then compared these ideas with what I really believe was right and good for myself and my family. I then joined the conservatives. I decided to join the side I was on."[1]

In the pages ahead, you will learn what it is to be an American and why it is important "to join the side you are on."

Brian Tracy

February 2012

CHAPTER 1

Patriotism

Sure, I wave the American flag. Do you know a better flag
to wave? Sure, I love my country with all her faults. I'm not
ashamed of that, never have been, never will be.

—John Wayne

Are You a Patriot?

Are you patriotic? Most Americans would answer that question with a resounding yes! But what does it really mean to be patriotic?

Thomas Jefferson once told a young boy who had been named after him to "love your neighbor as yourself, and your country more than yourself."[1] A patriot is someone who loves his country, who is willing to sacrifice for his country, and, yes, a patriot is someone willing to lay down his life for his country.

Are there many Americans nowadays who love their country so much that they are willing to make the ultimate sacrifice for its sake? Former Reagan speechwriter Peggy Noonan thinks there are—but also fears that their numbers are steadily diminishing. In a lecture to the Heritage Foundation, she observed that "we are living through the beginning of what I think is post-patriotic America. The ties that bind still exist, but they are growing frayed and tired and attenuated." She went on to indict our educational system for no longer fostering a sense of patriotism:

Nobody is really teaching our children to love their country. They still pick it up from their parents, from here and there, but in general, we have dropped the ball. The schools, most of them, do not encourage patriotic feeling. Small things—so many of them do not teach the Pledge of Allegiance. Bigger things—they do not celebrate Washington's birthday and draw pictures of him and hear stories about him as they did when we were kids. There is no Washington's birthday; there is President's Day, which my eleven-year-old son was once under the impression is a celebration of Bill Clinton's birthday.

Beyond that, the teaching of history has changed and has been altered all out of shape. My son is instructed far more in the sins of racism than in the virtues of Abe Lincoln. There is a school in Washington—and I almost moved there so my son could attend—that actually had pictures of Washington or Lincoln on the wall. On the wall of my son's classroom they had a big portrait of [Mexican artist] Frida Kahlo.[2]

And yet, there have been moments in our recent history when we have all set aside the pseudo-sophistication of "post-patriotic America" and come together as one in defense of what conservative thinker Russell Kirk called "the Permanent Things."

Remember back to where you were on that horrible eleventh day of September 2001. When the news of those terrorist attacks on our country ripped the needle off the record of your day, were there any of us mourning, angry, saddened, or gripped by any of the multitude of emotions sweeping the nation who thought of ourselves as Democrats or Republicans first? As the dust cleared and the tragedy began to sink in, was there anyone not feeling a sense of pride upon hearing the news that, despite the confusion and potential danger, our government, the House of Representatives, was gaveled into session by then Congressman Porter Goss to show those responsible that they could not destroy us? The House was only in session long enough to hear this prayer from Father Gerry Creedon: "God of peace and life, send Your Spirit to heal our country. Bring consolation to all injured in today's tragedy in New York and Washington. Protect us and help our leaders to lead us out of this moment of crisis to a new day of understanding and peace. Amen."[3]

A brief session, to be sure, but our government *was* in session—not running, not hiding. The fact that our representatives stood tall in that moment of confusion and fear and dared to enter that building, that chamber, assumed to be yet another target under attack, sent a message to the world that we would not be shaken, we would not cower, and we will not be defeated. That swell of pride you felt and feel is patriotism.

American Exceptionalism

Bred deep in the American psyche is the concept that the United States is a unique force for good in the world, a superpower that has not sought, and does not seek, to expand its borders through conquering and colonizing other lands. Secretary of State Colin Powell put it this way:

> We have sent men and women from the armed forces of the United States to other parts of the world throughout the last century to put down oppression. We defeated fascism, we defeated communism, we saved Europe in World War One and World War Two. . . . Did we ask for any land? No, the only land we ever asked for was enough land to bury our dead. That's the kind of nation we are.[4]

But it isn't simply our selfless actions that have made America unique; it's our core beliefs. Heritage scholar David Azerrad observed:

> To really understand what sets America apart, we need to examine the heart and soul of the nation: the ideas of the Declaration of Independence. Unlike other nations that derive their meaning and purpose from some unifying quality—an ethnic character, a common religion, a shared history, an ancestral land—America is a country dedicated to the universal ideas of equality and liberty. The truths we hold to be self-evident apply to *all men*—not just to all Americans. . . . In the most fundamental sense, America is an

exceptional nation not because of what it does—but because of what it *believes*.[5]

Because of America's dedication to the permanent truths expressed in the Declaration of Independence, our nation has a special responsibility to uphold the cause of liberty both at home and abroad. And while we have not always lived up to this responsibility, no nation has aspired so high and achieved so much as ours.

To cynical "post-patriotic" Americans, this may seem like an empty boast. Ronald Reagan's ambassador to the United Nations, Jeane Kirkpatrick, once noted that all too many Americans have fallen into the habit of "judging ourselves by the Sermon on the Mount, and everybody else on the curve."[6] But one need only look beyond oneself and try to see the world through the eyes of others—the eyes of those liberated from the oppression of Saddam Hussein or the eyes of Holocaust victims liberated by our troops—to recognize that they knew they were not trading one master for another; they were being set free.

In the eyes of the world, America stands for one thing above all: the promise of freedom. Even people who have never in their lives laid eyes on an American know of the promise of America, know that that promise means a better life, a life of freedom.

From the moment our Founding Fathers first put ink to the parchment that is the Declaration of Independence and pledged their lives, their fortunes, and their sacred honor to create this nation, that promise has come alive. If the Revolution had failed and the massive power of the British Empire prevailed over the colonists, the signers of the Declaration of Independence would have been rounded up, tried, and executed for treason against the Crown. Their properties and private fortunes would have been expropriated, and their families would have been left penniless and disgraced. When they made the commitment to stand together and break free of British rule in the name of liberty and independence, they were literally putting their lives on the line.

The roots of American liberty and patriotism were planted at the very beginning of the Republic. Each generation has been supported and nourished by the sacrifices and commitments of the patriotic Americans who have gone before it. And each generation has been charged with carrying the torch of liberty passed to it, keeping that flame alive as best it could before passing the torch forward, still burning brightly.

Subtly or overtly, each generation passes American exceptionalism to the next, be it through innovations like Henry Ford and his assembly line; or Thomas Edison and the light bulb; or Steve Jobs and the iPod, iPhone, and iPad; or through the encouraging words of parents to their children, assuring them that they can grow up to be anything they like if they put their minds to it and work hard. "Let the American youth never forget, that they possess a noble inheritance, bought by the toils, and sufferings, and blood of their ancestors," Supreme Court Justice Joseph Story said.[7] That's a lesson for all of us to remember.

The American Dream

The phrase "the American Dream" is used in many ways. When you look at the words carefully, they reveal something extraordinary. In all the history of man on earth, there has been only one country with the word *Dream* attached to it; there is only the American Dream. There is no French Dream or Russian Dream or Chinese Dream; there is only the American Dream, to which people from all over the world aspire and have aspired since our founding. People from 194 countries have come to America in order to participate in this dream.

What does the American Dream mean? Listen to what Indian-born Dinesh D'Souza told a Heritage audience in 2006:

> If I had remained in India I would probably have lived most of my life within a five-mile radius of where I was born. I would undoubtedly have married a woman of my identical religious, socioeconomic, and cultural background. I would almost certainly have become a medical doctor, an engineer, or a software programmer . . . In sum, my destiny would, to a large degree, have been given to me.
>
> . . . By coming to America, I have broken free from those traditional confines. . . . [A]t Dartmouth College . . . my reading included books like Plutarch's *Moralia, The Federalist Papers,* and Evelyn Waugh's *Brideshead Revisited.* They . . . implanted in my mind ideas that I had never previously considered. By the time I graduated, I had decided to become a writer, which is something you can do in America but which is not easy to do in India.
>
> After graduating . . . I became managing editor of a magazine and began writing freelance articles in newspapers. Someone in the Reagan administration was apparently impressed with my work, because I was called in

for an interview and hired as a senior domestic policy analyst. I found it strange to be working in the White House, because at the time I was not a United States citizen. I am sure that such a thing would not happen in India or anywhere else in the world. I also met my future wife during that time. [H]er ancestry is English, French, Scot-Irish, and German.

If there is a single phrase that encapsulates life in the Third World, it is that birth is destiny. . . . In America, by contrast, your destiny is not prescribed; it is constructed. Your life is like a blank sheet of paper, and you are the artist. The freedom to be the architect of your own destiny is the force behind America's worldwide appeal. Young people, especially, find the prospect of authoring the narrative of their own lives irresistible. So the immigrant, too, soon discovers that America will enable him to break free of the constraints that have held him captive while offering the future as a landscape of his own choosing.[8]

In America, people only care who you are, and they care little about your background. In America, you can start from anywhere, with or without benefits and advantages from your family, and make your own way and your own life. At any time, you can decide to change and do something completely different. Your life is yours to chart.

The American Dream of freedom, opportunity, and financial success is available to everyone who is willing to take the time and make the effort to learn how to achieve it. The only limits on individual achievement are those placed on individuals by themselves and their imaginations.

Remembering Who We Are

Jeane Kirkpatrick once said that "Americans need to face the truth about themselves, no matter how pleasant it is." And the truth is that the United States is an exceptional nation:

- It is the world's oldest and most stable capitalist democracy, older even than Great Britain, which did not become a mass democracy until the late nineteenth century.
- It is the first nation founded in an act of rebellion against a colonial power.
- It is the first nation founded on the belief that the rights of man are inherent and God given, and that the powers of government derive from the consent of the governed.
- It is the first nation to recognize that the powers of the state must be limited to those granted by the people and to recognize explicitly that the state was founded to secure their rights.
- It is the first nation to be based on a separation of powers—to prevent any branch of government from gaining too much power—and the clear subordination of the military to civilian rule.
- And it is the first nation to have codified all of these understandings in a Constitution that was publicly debated and democratically accepted.

Other nations share in some of these traditions, but precisely because the United States was founded—whereas nations such as England and France evolved—it stands, as the British writer G. K. Chesterton pointed out, as the only country in the world based on a creed. This creed sets us apart. Nobel laureate V. S. Naipaul said, America's creed "is an immense human idea. It cannot be reduced to a fixed system. It cannot generate fanaticism. But it is known to exist. And because of that, other more rigid systems in the end blow away."[9]

American patriotism is closely linked to American exceptionalism—to the belief that America's founding marked an immensely hopeful turning point in the history of mankind, a radically new beginning in which "common" men and women would finally come into their own and be empowered to pursue happiness in any way they saw fit, however crude or vulgar it might appear to their "betters." On the Fourth of July, amidst the barbecues and the fireworks, the games, the sales, and the hoopla, we Americans recall our country's founding, we renew our faith in its promise, and we offer up a silent prayer of thanks for living in this land of countless blessings and endless opportunities.

And just as we Americans celebrate the "immense human idea" behind our nation's founding, so should we remember that September day when we were attacked and members of Congress stood on the steps of the Capitol and pledged unity to bring those responsible to justice. Earlier generations have recalled Pearl Harbor, the USS *Maine*, Fort Sumter, or Lexington and Concord. Our generation will remember the night of September 11, when Republicans and Democrats, liberals and conservatives, spontaneously broke out into a chorus of "God Bless America" to show the world that despite our differences—and they are many, they are real, and they continue to this day—we are a family, we are one, and we will prevail.

That unity has subsequently been blurred by elections and the cut-and-thrust of politics, but patriotism and love of country live on in each of us, just below the surface. Never let us forget that day, and never let us forget that moment. And while, in the heat of political battle, we naturally focus on the differences between liberals and conservatives and their contrasting visions of our country's future, it is important to remember that regardless of party or political philosophy, we are Americans, we love our country, and we are patriots!

CHAPTER 2

Freedom

The God who gave us life, gave us liberty at the same time.

—Thomas Jefferson

Freedom

Throughout world history people have been oppressed, be it through slavery, by the state, by their sovereign or any number of entities that sought and succeeded to obtain and maintain power. From the start, America was different. While conquistadors first set foot in the Americas seeking only plunder, the first settlers, those who uprooted their lives and families to move here permanently, did so in the hope of escaping oppression of one form or another. Although they did not always live up to the lofty goals they set for themselves, they certainly planted the seed from which the tree of liberty grew.

President Abraham Lincoln opened the Gettysburg Address

this way: "Four score and seven years ago our fathers brought forth, upon this continent, a new nation, conceived in liberty, and dedicated to the proposition that 'all men are created equal.'" "Conceived in liberty." The irony and tragedy of slavery are not lost on us, but viewing history through the eyes of today cheapens the momentous achievements of a nation that, while not perfect, is ever striving toward the "more perfect Union" referenced in the preamble of the Constitution. Perfection is impossible to achieve; striving for it inspires greatness.

Ever since its founding, the United States has been, in the words of the late senator Daniel P. Moynihan (D-NY), the "party of liberty." The liberty we enjoy, that many of us take for granted and that oppressed masses around the world desperately seek, is part of our national DNA. It is the freedom to decide what to do with your life, how to live it, what career to pursue, what to think, and what to say. While anything but those options feels foreign to us, and the concept of not having those basic rights may be difficult, if not impossible, for us to imagine, they were simply concepts—abstract and interesting ideas—until the United States came into being.

The Magna Carta, written in 1215, first put limits on the power of a king and was an important precursor to our Constitution, but it was mainly a document that nobles forced King John of England to sign in order to protect their personal rights, not the rights of all men.

When our Constitution was ratified in 1789, for the first time in human history individual, God-given rights and a limited government went from concept to reality. "Liberty must at all hazards be supported. We have a right to it, derived from our

Maker. But if we had not, our fathers have earned and bought it for us, at the expense of their ease, their estates, their pleasure, and their blood," John Adams declared.[1]

Misconceptions About American Rights

The Constitution protects our God-given rights from government; the government does not grant those rights to us as citizens. This is perhaps the most widely misunderstood aspect of our system of government.

That the power of government is derived from the consent of the governed was first articulated by John Locke in his 1690 *Second Treatise of Government* when he wrote, "Men being, as has been said, by nature, all free, equal, and independent, no one can be put out of this estate, and subjected to the political power of another, without his own consent." Locke's words are the underlying basis of the First Amendment in the Bill of Rights, which reads: "Congress shall make no law respecting an establishment of religion, or prohibiting the free exercise thereof; or abridging the freedom of speech, or of the press; or the right of the people peaceably to assemble, and to petition the Government for a redress of grievances."

To hear a lot of people talk about it, they reference their First Amendment right to free speech as though the First Amendment grants them the right to say what they like. That is looking at it the wrong way.

Were the Constitution the granter of the right to free speech, religion, assembly, and so forth, the First Amendment would not start out, "Congress shall make no law." That part of the sentence clearly states that the government has no rightful authority over those things and is blocked from infringing upon them. This is the concept of negative rights.

A negative right is one that cannot be infringed upon by outside forces. Government is not granting you the right to free speech; it is expressly forbidden from attempting to infringe on it. While the saying "my constitutional right to free speech" may seem harmless, it points to a larger misunderstanding of where our rights come from.

The Declaration of Independence asserts that all men "are endowed by their Creator with certain unalienable Rights." In other words, our rights to "Life, Liberty, and the Pursuit of Happiness" are God given, not government given. But if you believe that we are granted our fundamental rights by the government, then you are more likely to seek additional favors from the government. If the government is the granter of all good things, what is to stop someone from thinking up more good things that could and should be granted by government?

Yet our government is not Santa Claus writ large, and our rights are not wish lists drawn up by eager tots on Christmas Eve. Any fair-minded reading of the Constitution reveals that it does not grant us the wonderful rights we embrace; it handcuffs the government from infringing upon them. Or at least, it used to be that way.

Nowhere do modern conservatives and liberals diverge more than on the reading of the Constitution and, therefore, on the origin of our most precious rights. Liberals view the Constitution as a living document that can have read into it nearly anything based on the political fashions of the day, so it is not surprising that someone like Senator Bernie Sanders (I-VT)—a self-described socialist—would pen a piece for the liberal *Huffington Post* titled "Health Care Is a Right, Not a Privilege."

Senator Sanders might be dismayed to learn that the totalitarian rulers of the former Soviet Union fully shared his commitment to health care as a fundamental right. Indeed, the Soviet Constitution guaranteed Soviet citizens the right to health care as well as a host of other rights—including the rights to labor, rest, material security in old age, housing, and education. For example: "USSR citizens have the right to labor—that is, to receive guaranteed work and remuneration for labor in accordance with its quantity and quality and not below the minimum amount established by the state. . . . This right is ensured by the socialist economic system, [and] the steady growth of productive forces."[2]

Of course, the Soviet Constitution could guarantee a job to every citizen because the state controlled the entire economy. There was no private sector. As long as you were a loyal Soviet citizen, the state would make sure that you had some sort of job, however poorly paid. But the moment you stepped out of line and criticized the state in any way, you would lose your state-run job, you would be hauled before a state-run court, and you would be sentenced to a state-run jail, a state-run mental home, or a state-run labor camp.

By contrast, although the media often refer to the president of the United States as the most powerful man in the world, in reality he lacks the power to tell even the smallest business owner whom to hire or fire. Admittedly our system has its drawbacks. Wouldn't it be convenient, for example, if an unemployed

American could simply call up a government bureaucrat and demand to be provided with his constitutionally guaranteed right to a job? On the other hand, because the government does not control the private sector in the United States, you and I are free to denounce the government on Monday, to demonstrate against government policy on Tuesday, to write an angry letter to the editor and post a blistering antigovernment blog on Wednesday, and not have to worry about losing our jobs on Thursday, appearing before a judge on Friday, and going to jail on Saturday.

Similarly, if the US government recognized a right to health care, it would be necessary for it to take control of the health-care industry, roughly 17 percent of our gross domestic product. How else could it enforce this right? Yet obtaining control of such a large slice of our economy would increase the powers of the state enormously and would pose a clear and present danger to our liberty. Indeed, the threat to American liberty posed by ObamaCare (a.k.a. the Patient Protection and Affordable Care Act) has led millions of heretofore politically uninvolved Americans to join the grassroots Tea Party movement.

The Tea Partiers' objections to ObamaCare are absolutely justified. By centralizing health-care decisions in Washington, ObamaCare places the federal government in charge of our most intensely personal matters: our own health care and the health care of our loved ones. Heritage scholar Robert Moffit has observed:

> Americans face a direct and historic challenge to their personal liberty and to their unique citizenship in a federal

republic. Through its enactment of the massive Patient Protection and Affordable Care Act, official Washington is not merely engineering a federal takeover of health care, but it is also radically altering the relationships between individuals and the government as well as the national government and the states.[3]

This is why conservatives steer clear of calling health care a right (implying greater government control in order to secure that right). Instead, we call for reforms that meet the health-care needs of both insured and uninsured Americans through greater reliance on the free market and the private sector. Conservatives also look to the states (which have already emerged as centers of resistance to the unprecedented concentration of political and economic power in Washington that is the essence of ObamaCare) to pursue high-quality, innovative health care.

Our Founding Fathers did not see government as a benevolent Santa Claus guaranteeing an ever-expanding wish list of rights; rather, they viewed government as a necessary evil—far preferable to anarchy, but nonetheless a serious threat to liberty. Liberty was the ultimate goal of our Founders, and for its sake they were willing to lay down their lives. In the famous words of Patrick Henry: "Is life so dear or peace so sweet as to be purchased at the price of chains and slavery? Forbid it, Almighty God! I know not what course others may take, but as for me, give me liberty, or give me death!"[4]

Patrick Henry's spirit—the American Spirit—continues to inspire oppressed peoples around the world. While the vicious dictatorship in Iran, for example, has remained steadfastly anti-American, the Iranian people themselves have warmed to the United States. This affection was not lost on that bastion of liberal media, the *Washington Post*, which ran a story in 2008 titled "Stars (and Stripes) in Their Eyes."[5] In it journalist Azadeh Moaveni recounts her shock at how average Iranian citizens reject their government's characterization of our way of life:

> Although their leaders still call America the "Great Satan," ordinary Iranians' affection for the United States seems to be thriving these days, at least in the bustling capital. This rekindled regard is evident in people's conversations, their insatiable demand for U.S. products and culture, and their fascination with the U.S. presidential campaign. One can't do reliable polling about Iranians' views under their theocratic government, of course, but these shifts were still striking to me as a longtime visitor.

That freedom and liberty seep into even the most oppressive regimes will come as no surprise to students of recent history. When the people of Eastern Europe rose up and regained their freedom and independence in 1989, the example of the United States inspired them. The masses embraced a democratic-capitalist system they had never known, embodied by what their government told them was the enemy of all peace-loving people—the United States. Our nation symbolized liberty to people who had never visited the United States and who were fed a daily diet of lies about us through government-controlled media. But liberty, like water, somehow finds a way.

Individual Liberty Under Siege

While the world's oppressed peoples have fought to move toward liberty and freedom, there are those in the United States who seek to deny it to their fellow citizens. Ironically they use freedom to undermine freedom.

Consider, for example, calls by the radical Left for the re-instatement of the so-called Fairness Doctrine. The Fairness Doctrine is an affront to freedom of speech. It requires radio and television stations to give equal time to opposing view-points, meaning that every hour of Rush Limbaugh must be countered with an hour devoted to the liberal viewpoint. The only problem is that Rush Limbaugh is wildly popular on radio, while the sum total of all liberal radio talk shows reaches only a fraction of his audience. Since radio (with the exception of National Public Radio) is a business, a profit must be made, and the only way to make it is by attracting as large an audi-ence as possible. Conservatives are extremely popular on radio. Progressives, despite many attempts and hundreds of millions of dollars, have not been able to break into radio in any meaning-ful way, so they seek to destroy talk radio instead. By denying stations hosting talk radio a profit, the Fairness Doctrine would accomplish precisely that.

But simply having the Federal Communications Commission reinstate the Fairness Doctrine without an understandable rea-son would expose these anti–free speech advocates for what they are—enemies of freedom—so a campaign of demonization is needed to justify their efforts. The radical community orga-nizer Saul Alinsky, in his handbook for left-wing extremists,

Rules for Radicals, laid out the framework for how modern leftists should attack their opponents, particularly in Rule 13: pick the target, freeze it, personalize it, and polarize it.

The accusations of racism against Rush Limbaugh, Sean Hannity, Mark Levin, Glenn Beck, and all other top-rated radio talk show hosts are as unfounded as they are unrelenting, but the Left's campaign of defamation is taken right out of Alinsky's playbook. By portraying conservative opponents as purveyors of hate speech, the Left seeks to limit their rights and the rights of the stations that carry their programs. Thus far, their campaign has been little more than a nuisance, but progressives are persistent. Their ultimate goal is to delegitimize all viewpoints except their own. Liberty, taken for granted by Americans, provides fertile ground for those seeking to eliminate it.

Personal Freedom and Economic Freedom

The freest societies throughout history have always been the most prosperous. The more freedom that people have to engage in entrepreneurial and other economic activities, the more products, processes, innovation, jobs, wealth, and opportunity will be created. History has shown that only in times of economic turmoil have the forces opposed to individual liberty been able to fully seize power. No revolution has overthrown a government in times of widely shared prosperity.

In the United States, the ten states noted for the greatest amount of freedom, opportunity, and encouragement of business activity are also the fastest-growing and most prosperous states. On the other hand, the states with the greatest burden of taxes, regulations, and restriction on businesses are the ten slowest-growing states.

The link between freedom and prosperity also holds true on the world's stage. For eighteen years now, the Heritage Foundation has produced the annual *Index of Economic Freedom* in cooperation with the editors of the *Wall Street Journal*. Each year, the *Index* ranks 179 nations in terms of their levels of economic freedom, characterizing them as "free," "mostly free," "moderately free," "mostly unfree," and "repressed." During this entire period, Hong Kong has always been ranked number one in the *Index*, thanks to its small government, low taxes, and light regulation. As former attorney general Edwin Meese— now a Distinguished Fellow at the Heritage Foundation—put it in a Heritage lecture, "Economic freedom and economic prosperity rise and fall together." Attorney General Meese cited the remarkable history of Hong Kong as a brilliant illustration of the value of political and economic freedom:

A century and a half ago, Britain's Lord Palmerston dismissed Hong Kong as "a barren rock with hardly a house upon it." One can only wonder what Lord Palmerston might think if he could visit Hong Kong today.

For he would walk among skyscrapers that hold the offices of nine thousand multinational companies. His eyes would behold the fifth-largest banking center on earth, and the eighth-largest stock market. He would stroll among citizens who earn the sixth-highest per capita income in the world. He would see a conduit through which flows 70 percent of all foreign investment in China. And he would no doubt be dumbstruck to see all this dynamic economic energy being generated on an island with a population smaller than that of Chicago.

Hong Kong's metamorphosis is all the more striking when you consider that it enjoys none of the natural resources that enabled other nations to become economic giants—no mighty rivers, no vast tracts of timber, no rich veins of ore and minerals. Yet, despite such handicaps, what Lord Palmerston called a "barren rock" is today the Pearl of the Orient—and a gleaming demonstration of the power and value of economic freedom.[6]

By contrast, nations like the United Kingdom and (alas!) the United States—once admired throughout the world for their commitment to economic freedom—have recently seen a sharp decline in their *Index* ratings. The director of Heritage's Center for International Trade and Economics, Ambassador Terry Miller, has noted:

For the U.S. and the U.K., the *Index of Economic Freedom* confirms what those countries' voters already knew, that there is an urgent need for real change. The U.S. dropped to 9th place in the 2011 *Index*, and the U.K. fell all the way to 16th place.

Those who feel we are losing economic vitality and leadership to Asia have cause for concern. Hong Kong, Singapore, Australia and New Zealand dominate the top of the economic freedom rankings. Economic growth rates in those countries averaged 6.8 percent in 2010.

. . . Politicians around the world are getting the message, or they are being replaced. The proven path to prosperity is the path of freedom. Individuals want control of their own lives. They want governments that facilitate, not czars that coerce or command. Fortunately, the process of reclaiming our economic freedom has already begun. Our economic recovery depends on its rapid success.[7]

It is important to note that the 2012 *Index of Economic Freedom* by the Heritage Foundation found little changed in the top of the list. The same four countries reside there along with newcomer Switzerland. The entire list can be found at www. Heritage.org. Ambassador Miller's commentary on the findings of the *Index of Economic Freedom* reinforces the eloquent words with which Attorney General Meese concluded his 1999 Heritage lecture: "To attain freedom is mankind's highest aspiration. To use freedom wisely is mankind's urgent responsibility. To preserve freedom is mankind's continuing challenge. May we all be equal to that task."[8]

CHAPTER 3

Individuality

> Whatever crushes individuality is despotism, whether it professes to be enforcing the will of God or the injunctions of men.
>
> —John Stuart Mill

Individuality

Nothing encapsulates the American Spirit more than individuality. Our Founding Fathers brought into being a nation where individuals are free to choose their own lives and destinies.

When Benjamin Franklin was leaving the Constitutional Convention on September 18, 1787, an excited, curious, and anxious crowd met him. Mrs. Powel of Philadelphia asked him, "Well, Doctor, what have we got, a republic or a monarchy?" Franklin's answer was both hopeful and a warning to Mrs.

Powel and the waiting crowd. "A republic, if you can keep it," he said.[1]

By rejecting a monarchy—one that would have been easy to sell to a public that had really known nothing else, having been subjects of King George III only a few years earlier, and having a ready-made king in George Washington—the Founding Fathers not only enshrined our liberties in law but also fanned the smoldering embers of our natural individuality to the point that they became a roaring, eternal flame.

The republican form of government had mostly been consigned to the history books since the fall of Rome. Monarchies had ruled the leading powers of the world for centuries. By choosing a republic, where the governed control the government, not the other way around, the Founding Fathers displayed faith in the individual's ability to know better than any elected or appointed official what is best for himself and his family. The American people, since that day, have justified that faith time and again.

Innovation and the entrepreneurial spirit, while possible in other countries, have found a home in the United States. This was no accident. Nick A. Adams, an Australian student of the United States, wrote,

> It may surprise Americans to learn that in many Western cultures, in countries extremely similar to their own, successful people are criticized, resented and targeted. These cultures do not like or reward people whose talents or achievements distinguish them. . . . Being different by exhibiting individuality and independence in these countries is not the way to

get ahead in life. Self-promotion is considered the gravest of sins and the poorest of forms. The contrast could not be starker.[2]

Individuality is the lifeblood of creativity, and nowhere on earth has creativity thrived as it has in America. In part, that's because "individuality is the aim of political liberty," James Fenimore Cooper explained. "By leaving to the citizen as much freedom of action and of being, as comports with order and the rights of others, the institutions render him truly a freeman. He is left to pursue his means of happiness in his own manner."[3]

Each person, at each stage of life, is shaped by the dominant social codes and cultural expectations of his environment. In societies with feudal backgrounds, such as those in Europe, with their many-layered class distinctions, a strong set of social expectations represses the individuality of children from an early age. In America, however, things are different and better. Americans are individual and distinct in thinking, in acting, and in expressing their personalities. This expression of individuality is encouraged and rewarded at every level of American society and throughout life. We see this especially in sports and show business, where uniquely talented personalities are some of the most admired and respected people in our society.

"In America," said Thomas Jefferson, "no other distinction between man and man had ever been known but that of persons in office exercising powers by authority of the laws, and private individuals. Among these last, the poorest laborer stood on equal ground with the wealthiest millionaire, and generally on a more favored one whenever their rights seem to jar."[4]

From Rags to Riches

In America it makes no difference where you start out in life; your life is what you make of it. More captains of industry have risen from humble beginnings here than in any other nation on earth. Perhaps the greatest rags-to-riches story in modern history is that of Andrew Carnegie, who went from poverty in Scotland to become one of the richest men in the world.

Carnegie moved to the United States at age thirteen with his family in pursuit of a better life. Andrew worked in a cotton mill earning a mere $1.20 per week in 1848. By 1853 he was earning $4.00 per week working as a telegraph operator for the Pennsylvania Railroad Company where he began to excel and rapidly work his way up the corporate ladder. At that time he began investing in stocks.

Through his investments, fueled by his self-education, Carnegie formed the Carnegie Steel Company. Thanks to his innovations in the production of steel, his company grew exponentially. In 1901 he sold the Carnegie Steel Company to J. P. Morgan for the staggering sum of $480 million, and the company became US Steel.

At the time of the sale Andrew Carnegie was the second-richest man in the world—not bad for a poor immigrant boy. He spent the rest of his life engaged in some of the greatest philanthropy the world has ever seen, giving away his fortune to found and fund libraries, universities, and philanthropic ventures around the world. The ultimate self-starter, Carnegie said, "People who are unable to motivate themselves must be content with mediocrity, no matter how impressive their other talents."

Americans are encouraged to follow their hearts and fulfill their dreams, and those dreams are as diverse as each person. Whether someone attains her dreams remains up to her, but the ability to aspire, coupled with the possibility of achieving her aspirations, remains a major driving force behind the American Spirit.

The old saw that parents tell their children, "You can grow up to be anything you want," is uniquely American. Until the founding of the United States the odds of a person rising from the lowest to the highest station in life were virtually nil, with the exception of those rising and seizing power through military means. But in America that saying is true.

Starting with Andrew Jackson, who was born into poverty, was orphaned during the Revolutionary War, and rose to become commander of American forces at the Battle of New Orleans, and eventually the seventh president of the United States, we have a history of individuals overcoming the odds to achieve great things. In recent history, two of the last five US presidents—Ronald Reagan and Bill Clinton—rose from poverty to lead the most powerful nation on earth. In his 1981 Inaugural Address, Reagan said, "I do not believe in a fate that will fall on us no matter what we do. I do believe in a fate that will fall on us if we do nothing." Reagan wasn't talking about his amazing journey from poverty to 1600 Pennsylvania Avenue, but he might have been.

Luck is an important ingredient of any success, but luck alone will not carry anyone through to victory.

The Individual Spirit

Anyone who has achieved greatness on any level will tell you that his success was not an accident, not simply luck, but a product of hard work combined with opportunity and experience. No matter how similar their circumstances or accomplishments, no two people ever take the same path through life. The unique experiences we live through shape our individual characters.

How we deal with failure is as important as how we deal with success. Where many would be discouraged by failure, the truly successful are not deterred. Thomas Edison, perhaps the most prolific inventor in world history, when asked about his many failed attempts to create an electric light bulb reportedly said, "I have not failed, I've just found ten thousand ways that won't work."

That attitude is distinctly American. Edison eventually did create his light bulb and hundreds of other inventions. His perseverance was rewarded. "Many of life's failures are people who did not realize how close they were to success when they gave up," Edison said on the subject.

With rare exceptions like the printing press, the greatest innovations, inventions, and discoveries in human history have come since the founding of the United States and in the United States. The power of the individual inspires human beings. When that individuality is stifled by government, when government controls the individual, creativity slows and goes underground.

Unfortunately, government naturally tends to expand its

own power. This expansion necessarily comes at the price of individual liberty and, therefore, the price of creativity. But government cares little if creativity suffers; it perpetually seeks more control, more power. And growing government power means more power to interfere with, to have influence or control over, more and more of a citizen's life.

The Founders were quite aware of government's tendency to interfere in the lives, work, business, and finances of others. They designed the Constitution with strict prohibitions on the busybodies and meddlers, especially those who got into public office or positions of authority. They established strict checks and balances in the executive, the legislative, and the judicial branches of government to protect the average person from the arbitrary opinions and impositions of others.

The Constrained Vision

One of the most important formative influences in the lives of the Founding Fathers and the debates over the Declaration of Independence and Constitution was the acknowledgment of human nature and natural law. The Founding Fathers believed that there were certain unalterable characteristics of people and society and that a proper system of governance had no choice but to accept them and provide for them in the laws.

This approach strongly contradicted the idea that human beings were like lumps of clay that could be shaped and formed by government policy. Indifference to the fundamental nature of people led ultimately to the emergence of totalitarianism and to the illusion that government edicts could create a "new man."

Dictators and tyrants were convinced they could force people to become passive, compliant members of a vast human collective. Ideas of unlimited state power have been totally discredited today, especially by the testimonies of people who were made to live under real socialism and know how horrible it really was. They survive today mainly in such intellectual and political backwaters as North Korea and Cuba. Curiously they also are alive and well on many American campuses, where a reactionary professoriate desperately clings to the Marxist clichés and illusions of an earlier era.

Our approach to human nature is based on what economist and social philosopher Thomas Sowell calls "the constrained vision." This approach to human affairs recognizes "the moral limitations of man in general, and his egocentricity in particular."[5] The Founders had a constrained vision of humanity's potential, brilliantly summarized by James Madison in *Federalist* 51: "If men were angels, no government would be necessary. If angels were to govern men, neither external nor internal controls on government would be necessary." But men are not angels. Human beings are motivated by a variety of emotions, including greed, envy, ambition, self-interest, impatience, and desire for personal gain. This fundamental constraint never changes. Instead of trying to modify or reshape the basic qualities of human nature, the Founding Fathers set up a system within which self-interested individuals would have to compete and cooperate with others to achieve their goals.

America is great because the foundations of American exceptionalism and American individualism are built into the fabric of our nation. The Founders held a vision of an America made up of an unlimited number of individuals who would come together, within a framework of law, order, and good government, to create a nation that would be unique in all the history of the world. They summarized this in the motto *E Pluribus Unum*, which means "out of many—one." The unique characters, personalities, talents, and abilities of all these people would form a single nation that would be truly universal, open to all mankind.

Adversity and Individuality

The late author and paleontologist Stephen Gould once said, "I am somehow less interested in the weight and convolutions of Einstein's brain than in the near certainty that people of equal talent have lived and died in cotton fields and sweatshops."[6] Gould's observation is undoubtedly true. Throughout history, many gifted people have been crushed by misfortune and never had the opportunity to exercise their talents. What separates success from failure is how an individual transcends the circumstances that confront him.

Richard Nixon lost the presidential election in 1960 to John F. Kennedy, then went on to lose his bid for governor of California in 1962. While faced with unimaginable disappointment, Nixon told the press, "You won't have Nixon to kick around anymore." Discouraged by two successive losses, he planned to return to private life and put the prospect of public rejection behind him forever. But his unique personal qualities would not allow him simply to fade away, and he returned to public life and was elected president in 1968.

Although his presidency ended in disgrace, Nixon never

did fade away. He spent his life writing books, giving speeches, and influencing public policy and debate. Something inside him wouldn't accept where he was; he wanted to do more and to be more.

The history of the United States is filled with stories of individuals overcoming adversity that, had they lived elsewhere in the world, would have held them captive in the circumstances into which they were born.

Jim Abbott, like many boys, loved baseball. But Jim was different. Born in Flint, Michigan, in 1967, he seemed unlikely to grow and play Little League baseball, let alone make it to the major leagues. Jim was born without a right hand, so playing a sport that required every appendage seemed a bridge too far to be realized. Someone forgot to convince Jim of that.

Jim *wanted* to play baseball and be a pitcher, so he set about practicing. He developed a system by which he could deliver a pitch and have his glove in a ready position by the time the ball crossed the plate. Jim was good. He was so good, in fact, that he was drafted out of high school by the Toronto Blue Jays, but instead opted for college at the University of Michigan. While at the university, Jim led the Wolverines to two Big Ten championships, and he was the first baseball pitcher to be awarded the James E. Sullivan Award as amateur athlete of the year in 1987. It was a major accomplishment for anyone, let alone someone with only one hand. But Jim wasn't finished yet.

After his amazing college career, Jim was drafted in the first round by the California Angels and spent the next ten years living out the dream of every little boy who ever played on a sandlot. What's more, Jim joined the exclusive club of pitchers who have ever thrown a no-hitter when, in 1993, he blanked the Cleveland Indians.

When you first hear his story, without being told that Jim Abbott was born with only one hand, you would never know it, never even think it. But once the surprise of his story wears off, it gives way to an acknowledgment that it makes perfect sense because Jim Abbott is an American and America is all about amazing stories.

Each story of an individual seizing the opportunities presented to him or creating his own opportunities through his choices is a testament to a nation that values individual liberty and ingenuity. Only in a society that values the individual will someone like Clarence Thomas—a descendant of slaves, born into poverty and segregation—have the opportunity to become an associate justice of the Supreme Court of the United States.

Individuality Under Siege

In recent years, however, government policy has focused on the needs of socially disadvantaged groups rather than on individuals. A 2004 Congressional Research Service (CRS) survey of federal affirmative action policies, for example, found some 173 "goals, timetables, set-asides, and quotas" in virtually every area where the federal government hires employees, allocates contracts, dispenses benefits, or enacts regulations. As the Heritage Foundation's vice president for government relations, Mike Franc, has noted, "The set-asides come in all shapes and sizes—5 percent, 6.9 percent, 8 percent, 10 percent, 12 percent, and even 15 percent."

And who is eligible to benefit from these provisions? "There are as many answers," Franc wrote,

> as there are federal agencies and statutory schemes. My favorite is the definition of "socially disadvantaged" in the Small Business Administration's 8(a) program. . . . Groups presumed to be "socially disadvantaged" include: "Black Americans; Hispanic Americans; Native Americans (American Indians, Eskimos, Aleuts, or Native Hawaiians); Asian Pacific Americans (persons with origins from Burma, Thailand, Malaysia, Indonesia, Singapore, Brunei, Japan, China (including Hong Kong), Taiwan, Laos, Cambodia (Kampuchea), Vietnam, Korea, The Philippines, U.S. Trust Territory of the Pacific Islands (Republic of Palau), Republic of the Marshall Islands, Federated States of Micronesia, the Commonwealth of the Northern Mariana Islands, Guam, Samoa, Macao, Fiji, Tonga, Kiribati, Tuvalu or Naru); Subcontinent Asian Americans (persons with origins from India, Pakistan, Bangladesh, Sri Lanka, Bhutan, the Maldive Islands, or Nepal)" and members of other groups as designated by the SBA from time to time.
>
> Got that? Even those with ties to Hong Kong, Taiwan, South Korea and Singapore, which rank among the world's most affluent and economically free economies, are deemed "socially disadvantaged."[7]

But the new emphasis on group rights is not merely illogical; it is profoundly divisive. Former deputy secretary of education Eugene Hickok has pointed out, "The assertion of group rights involves claims being made by one group against another, which invariably involves inequalities and making distinctions among people. It is an approach to rights which forces people to dwell on what they do not have in common, undermining any deeper sense of community that might come to shape the contours of our politics."[8]

In a May 2007 interview with ABC's George Stephanopoulos, then Senator Barack Obama declared that affirmative action "can't be a quota system and it can't be something that is simply applied without looking at the whole person, whether that person is black or white or Hispanic, male or female." He even held out the hope that affirmative action would eventually wither away, becoming "a diminishing tool to achieve racial equality in this society."

Now that an African American occupies the Oval Office, isn't it time to eliminate the race-based, gender-based, and group-based preferences currently embedded in federal laws? In America, individuality is enshrined in the very fabric of our being. It allows each of us to make what we will of our lives and has been the incubator of the world's greatest inventions and innovations. Only by returning to our long-standing belief that we are a nation of individuals limited merely by our imaginations, and not by the government, will we continue to reap the harvest of creativity and prosperity that our system is uniquely suited to foster.

CHAPTER 4

Responsibility

It is time to restore the American precept that each
individual is accountable for his actions.

—Ronald Reagan

Responsibility

Every parent has heard "I didn't do it" from a child standing
over something broken. Avoiding punishment for wrong-
doing is a normal reaction from a child, but instilling personal
responsibility in children so they are ready for adulthood is a
major goal of parenting. Striving to achieve that goal is the key
to a civil society and personal success.

Responsibility, personal or professional, is a very American
trait. Harry Truman famously kept a sign that read "The Buck
Stops Here" on his desk in the White House. Our history is
filled with examples of people, from famous politicians and

celebrities to people you've never heard of, stepping up and exercising personal responsibility when not doing so would have been the easier choice. Acting responsibly, even when no one is looking, serves as the glue of civil society.

Personal Responsibility

The United States was founded on a doctrine of personal responsibility; the Declaration of Independence was a statement of just that. Each of the fifty-six signers of the Declaration knew the risk he was taking. Sticking their thumbs in the eye of the most powerful man on earth seemed the height of folly at the time. They knew King George would send an army, a huge and formidable force, to quash their insurrection and keep his British Empire intact.

The safe path when faced with odds of that sort would have been to issue the Declaration anonymously, hope things went the way they wanted, and if they didn't, pray their anonymity held or run for their lives. But cowardice was not in the character of our Founding Fathers.

Despite the risks, risks noted by Benjamin Franklin in his remark, "We must all hang together, or assuredly we shall all hang separately," they put quill to parchment and told King George, told the world, what they were doing, why they were doing it, and most shockingly who they were.

Knowing they were putting their lives on the line, they acknowledged that fact in the closing of the document: "And for the support of this Declaration, with a firm Reliance on the protection of divine Providence, we mutually pledge to each other our Lives, our Fortunes, and our sacred Honor." Although personal responsibility rarely requires you to stand up to a tyrant or risk your life, it does require the same character traits displayed by our Founding Fathers.

Later, George Washington pointed out, "It is . . . [the citizens'] choice, and depends upon their conduct, whether they will be respectable and prosperous, or contemptible and miserable as a Nation. This is the time of their political probation; this is the moment when the eyes of the World are turned upon them."[1]

The acceptance of responsibility is an essential prerequisite of leadership in every area. It is a quality of exceptional people. It is difficult to imagine an authentic leader, a successful businessperson, or a person of any moral consequence who does not accept responsibility for his actions.

Why Responsibility Matters

Responsibility is often used with a negative connotation, as in "he was responsible for the deaths of thousands," but Americans build a more prosperous and just society by taking responsibility for one another.

Taking responsibility for one another means, first and foremost, providing for one's family. Strong, thriving families are not only desirable in themselves; they're the building blocks of American prosperity. Stephen Moore, senior economics writer for the editorial board of the *Wall Street Journal*, observed:

A failing economy puts stress on families. . . . If families are split apart by economic hardship, this will be a bigger blow to the long-term economy than even lost wealth. Why? Because healthy, intact, and loving families are absolutely critical to keeping the U.S. economy on solid footing in future years and decades.

I will not summarize all the evidence here, but suffice it to say that . . . [t]he convenient mythology that divorce and out-of-wedlock births have little lasting impact on children has now been exposed as devastatingly inaccurate. Children in single-parent homes generally have lower self-esteem, more drug use, lower academic achievement and higher rates of depression than children in two-parent homes. What is more, longitudinal studies now suggest that these effects are long-lasting. Children who grow up in intact families with both spouses present in the home have higher educational achievement and higher incomes than children from broken families.

In other words, if we want our economy to perform, we need our families to be resilient and stable.[2]

Besides taking responsibility for their families, Americans have always offered a helping hand to neighbors in distress. Frequently they act through faith-based organizations. Consider the case of Cheryl and Ron Murff. In 2006, a local Dallas minister asked them to give not only of their money but also of their time to help the less fortunate. Cheryl and Ron agreed. Heritage scholar Ryan Messmore explained what happened next:

Every Saturday since then, Cheryl and Ron drive to South Dallas to spend time with Rodrick and Lisa. A few years ago,

Rodrick was a drug dealer controlling 70 percent of the drug traffic in his neighborhood. He had frequent run-ins with the law, fathered four children out of wedlock, and lived with his girlfriend Lisa in an apartment in a public-housing project. One night when he found his four-year old son imitating him by rolling up a piece of paper like a joint, Rodrick reached a breaking point. He knew he had to change his life around, and he turned to a Christian ministry for help.

Faith-based organizations play an essential role in helping to connect those in need with resources and relationships that transform lives. Mike Fechner, the head of a ministry called H.I.S. BridgeBuilders, helped Rodrick kick drugs, get married to Lisa, and participate in a Bible study. It was Mike who also challenged Cheryl with taking time for the poor. When she asked how she and her husband could make a difference in combating poverty in Dallas, Mike suggested they cultivate a personal relationship with Rodrick and Lisa. Equipped with no special training or skills except a desire to serve others, Cheryl and Ron agreed.

At first, the two couples simply spent time together getting to know each other. It didn't take long, though, for Cheryl and Ron to understand some of the real difficulties facing their new friends. With Rodrick's police record, it was hard for him to get a job, and he was being asked to give up his steady stream of income from selling drugs. He couldn't afford a big car, but he couldn't fit his kids' four car seats in the vehicle that he had.

Together, the couples began to develop an unconventional friendship that would change their lives. Cheryl and

Ron helped Rodrick financially and in other ways—modeling good habits and showing how a mutually supportive marriage can work. But the relationship wasn't a one-way street. Cheryl and Ron learned just as much in return, especially about sustaining joy and gratitude during life's ups and downs. Today the couples can be found going out on double dates and sharing Thanksgiving dinner. When asked how long she plans to continue this kind of relationship, Cheryl responds without hesitation: "Forever!"[3]

The results have been spectacular. Rodrick is now on the staff of H.I.S. BridgeBuilders ministry. He is married to Lisa, works hard to support his family and be a good role model for his children, and even provides hope for others living in poverty and addiction. He and his children are no longer the responsibility of others in the welfare state.

Unfortunately as the welfare state has grown ever larger, Americans' sense of responsibility for their own well-being and for that of their families and neighbors appears to have grown smaller. Some Americans have come to regard the government as their first line of defense, responsible for defending them even against the ordinary vicissitudes of daily life, however minor. Consider the following verbatim call from a citizen to a 911 dispatcher in Orange County, California:

DISPATCHER: Sheriff's department, how can I help you?
CALLER: Yeah, I'm over here at Burger King, right here
    in San Clemente—
DISPATCHER: Mm-hmm.

CALLER: Um, no, not San Clemente, I'm sorry. Um, I live in San Clemente. I'm in Laguna Niguel, I think that's where I'm at.

DISPATCHER: Uh-huh.

CALLER: I'm at a drive-thru right now.

DISPATCHER: Uh-huh.

CALLER: I ordered my food three times. They're mopping the floor inside, and I understand they're busy. They're not even busy, okay, I've been the only car here. I asked them four different times to make me a Western Barbecue Burger. Okay, they keep giving me a hamburger with lettuce, tomato, and cheese, onions. And I said, I am not leaving.

DISPATCHER: Uh-huh.

CALLER: I want a Western Burger. Because I just got my kids from tae kwon do; they're hungry. I'm on my way home, and I live in San Clemente.

DISPATCHER: Uh-huh.

CALLER: Okay, she gave me another hamburger. It's wrong. I said four times, I said, "I want it." She goes, "Can you go out and park in front?" I said, "No. I want my hamburger right." So then the lady came to the manager, or whoever she is—she came up and said, "Um, did you want your money back?" And I said, "No. I want my hamburger. My kids are hungry, and I have to jump on the toll freeway [sic]." I said, "I am not leaving this spot," and I said I will call the police, because I want my Western Burger done right. Now is that so hard?

DISPATCHER: Okay, what exactly is it you want us to do for you?

CALLER: Send an officer down here. I want them to make me the right—

DISPATCHER: Ma'am, we're not going to go down there and enforce your Western Bacon Cheeseburger.

CALLER: What am I supposed to do?

DISPATCHER: This is between you and the manager. We're not going to enforce how to make a hamburger. That's not a criminal issue. There's nothing criminal there.

CALLER: So I just stand here—so I just sit here and block—

DISPATCHER: You need to calmly and rationally speak to the manager and figure out what to do between you.

CALLER: She did come up, and I said, "Can I please have my Western Burger?" She said, "I'm not dealing with it," and she walked away. Because they're mopping the floor, and it's all full of suds, and they don't want to go through there, and—

DISPATCHER: Ma'am, then I suggest you get your money back and go somewhere else. This is not a criminal issue. We can't go out there and make them make you a cheeseburger the way you want it.

CALLER: Well, that is, that—you're supposed to be here to protect me.

DISPATCHER: Well, what are we protecting you from, a wrong cheeseburger?

CALLER: No, it's . . .

DISPATCHER: Is this, like, is this a harmful cheeseburger or something? I don't understand what you
want us to do.

CALLER: Well, just come down here! I'm not leaving!

DISPATCHER: No ma'am, I'm not sending the depu-
ties down there over a cheeseburger! You need to
go in there and act like an adult and either get your
money back or go home.

CALLER: I do not need to go. She is not acting like
an adult herself. I'm sitting here in my car. I
just want them to make me a Western Burger
[unintelligible].

DISPATCHER: Now this is what I suggest: I suggest you
get your money back from the manager, and you go
on your way home.

CALLER: Okay.

DISPATCHER: Okay? Bye-bye.

CALLER: No . . .

[*click*][4]

Nobel laureate F. A. Hayek warned in *The Road to Serfdom*,
the "most important change which extensive government control produces is a psychological change, an alteration in the
character of the people."[5]

Stories of Americans Acting Responsibly

Of course, not every abdication of responsibility will lead
to absurdities like the 911 call just cited. Nonetheless, the

withering of personal responsibility can devastate individuals, families, and even nations. That is why it is important to celebrate acts of responsibility when they occur and to pass those lessons on to future generations, so we do not repeat the mistakes of the past.

Investment advisor Bernie Madoff, in the largest Ponzi scheme in history, bilked thousands of investors out of billions of dollars, bankrupting countless individuals and pension funds. With little hope of recovering more than a fraction of the money stolen, people had their lives destroyed.

One victim of the Madoff thievery was the Robert I. Lappin Charitable Trust, having lost the $8 million it invested with Madoff. The trust, founded in 1993 by Robert Lappin to create and run programs for Jewish youth in Massachusetts, was forced to temporarily shut its doors. It lost the retirement savings of its employees and employees of other Lappin family ventures. But Robert Lappin had made a promise to those employees and felt a sense of responsibility to keep his word. In an act he was in no way legally obligated to do, Robert Lappin and his family donated $5 million to restore the stolen funds and restore the retirement that sixty people had had stolen from them.

Lappin had lost a significant portion of his family's personal wealth to Bernie Madoff, and yet he donated what amounted to more than half his remaining net worth to keep his word, to fulfill his responsibilities. His son Peter told the *Boston Globe* that the decision to make right what was wronged was an easy one for his father and family. Robert knew it was the right thing to do, joking with the *Globe* about the reaction of his former employees to the gift: "At least from the feedback, they feel very grateful and happy, which makes me feel very happy. So far no kisses, but I have had some hugs."[6]

Stepping up and doing the right thing can be as simple as admitting a mistake, even if the admission is a difficult one. On June 2, 2010, Detroit Tigers pitcher Armando Galarraga was on the verge of the rarest pitching feat in baseball, a perfect game. He had retired the first twenty-six batters he faced, needing only one more out to become the twenty-first person in the history of the game to achieve perfection. On a ground ball to the first baseman, Galarraga covered the base and caught the ball, and the runner was out, perfection. The crowd went wild, Galarraga raised his arms in triumph, and then shock came over all of them. The runner was called safe; the perfection was only almost.

A replay showed the runner was out and not just by a little, but clearly. First base umpire Jim Joyce had gotten the call wrong. Armando had lost not only his perfect game but also a no-hitter. Retiring the next batter, Galarraga became one of many pitchers in history to throw a one-hitter. But that was not the end of the story.

Umpire Jim Joyce, a twenty-two-year veteran, saw the replay and knew he had made the mistake that Armando's teammates and coach and the thousands of fans had accused him of. The easy thing to do would have been to slip out of the stadium and accept the offer made by Major League Baseball to skip the rest of the games in Detroit in order to avoid facing angry fans. But Joyce is a professional and a man of character. He wasn't going to avoid what had happened.

Joyce went to Armando Galarraga that night, admitted his mistake, and apologized. He did the same in the press. The rage that was boiling in the media, on the Internet, and with fans across the country was immediately defused. By stepping up and taking responsibility, rather than being obstinate or evasive, Jim Joyce went from goat to hero almost immediately. He was praised in the press and cheered the next day at the game when he stayed to umpire behind home plate. When Galarraga and Joyce, with tears in his eyes and obviously distraught by his error, met on the field, they embraced.

As with many events in sports, memories quickly fade as attentions turn to the latest news or scandal, and this event is no different. But when people speak of it now, immediately after the phrase "blown call" is uttered, it is followed by Joyce's admission. Any anger or outrage remaining is leveled toward Major League Baseball itself for not reversing the call and granting Galarraga the perfect game, which is well within its power.

Jim Joyce is not the punch line of jokes or the focus of anger or derision. He is an example to be held up as how people should be—all because he took responsibility for his mistake.

Not every act of responsibility requires wealthy individuals donating millions of dollars or someone making a public admission of a mistake. To take responsibility simply requires someone, or a group of people, to do the right thing.

On September 12, 2009, citizens from all corners of the United States went to Washington, DC, for a rally. Estimates of the crowd's size vary, but photos and calculations suggest that the number reached well into six figures. A river of protesters marched down Pennsylvania Avenue and packed the east end of the National Mall to hear speakers on the Capitol terrace. This crowd bristled with messages about responsibility and other traditional American values. When asked by reporters what message they wanted to send to Congress, protesters most frequently said, "Stop spending money you don't have! Don't leave a huge debt for our children and grandchildren to pay!"

Walking among the crowd that Saturday, one saw America at its best. These were ordinary, hardworking people. They bought their own bus and plane tickets, paid their own hotel tabs, and made their own signs. Many came as families: parents, grandparents, and children. Senior citizens and military veterans were everywhere. They radiated good cheer among themselves and outrage toward their government. They were fed up with politicians squandering their taxes and appropriating powers not found in the Constitution. And they said so, all day long. The behavior of the September 12 crowd also spoke clearly. Without being told to, they treated the nation's front lawn like it was their own. They took responsibility for their actions. When the sun rose on Sunday, September 13, people strolling on the National Mall saw something remarkable. There was no litter. No paper, no bottles, no cans, no signs, no placards. Just acres of green grass.

Into everyone's life a little responsibility must fall; it's whether you take it that defines you. History's greatest tragedies are riddled with examples of people abdicating their responsibility to authority. Thankfully our Founding Fathers instilled personal responsibility into our psyche as a nation in the very act of our founding, but it's up to each of us to keep it alive and pass it on to future generations.

Former House Speaker Newt Gingrich told a Heritage audience in 1998:

> I would argue that responsibility may well be at the heart of liberty and at the heart of freedom and at the heart of survival. If you do not have a sense of responsibility inculcated in your citizens, you cannot be free. If everybody sitting in those ships off the shore of Normandy had said "not me," Europe today would be dominated by the Nazis. If everybody who had to raise children said "not me," we would live in a world of barbarians in one generation. If everybody who had to go to work said "not me," there would be no wealth to redistribute. The great challenge to our liberal friends is this: If no one is responsible enough to create wealth, how will we give it away?[7]

Passing responsibility along is easy. It starts with you. As individuals, Americans take responsibility for their lives by living within their means and providing for their families. As parents, Americans help out with the homework, attend parent-teacher conferences, and teach by example. As members of a community, Americans engage in countless acts of kindness in good times and (especially) in bad. And as citizens, whenever politicians put forward new schemes to "help out" by transferring more of life's responsibilities to Washington, Americans can recall Ronald Reagan's typically insightful observation. "The nine most terrifying words in the English language," Reagan said, "are, 'I'm from the government and I'm here to help.'"

English writer G. K. Chesterton called the United States "a nation with the soul of a church." Taking responsibility for ourselves, our families, and our neighbors defines the American soul and lends grace, goodness, and dignity to the American Spirit.

CHAPTER 5

Optimism

Optimism is the faith that leads to achievement. Nothing
can be done without hope and confidence.

—Helen Keller

Optimism

The United States is the land of optimism. We were settled by
the ultimate optimists, people willing to risk their lives during a
dangerous three-month sea voyage in the hope of a better life in
a land they had never laid eyes on. Throughout our history, we
have served as a beacon of hope to oppressed men and women
everywhere.

For generations, native-born and immigrant Americans
alike have believed that they could create a better way of life and
fashion a better future for themselves and their descendants.
And they've been proven correct time and again. Our inherent

optimism is alive and well in every man, woman, and child in the country, to one degree or another. That optimism is a key component to our future success as individuals and as a nation.

America was settled by men and women who had to give up everything—leaving family, friends, language, and culture behind—cross the ocean, and start life anew in a foreign land, often with little more than pluck, determination, and a belief in a Supreme Being. These new immigrants and pioneers had to be incredible optimists, just to overcome the inertia and resistance of leaving everything behind.

Later immigrants came packed into third-class berths on steamships. Most understood they were making a one-way trip. They'd never see their homelands or their families again. Yet they were willing to take that risk and endure a dangerous trip because they optimistically believed a better life awaited them.

Their basic premise was that a transcendent and eternal God, not capricious political government, gave them their freedom. Under this providential dispensation, it was possible, by willingly undertaking incredible risks, to create a new life in a new world. No matter how many problems they endured when arriving in America, they never lost sight of the idea of America's greatness. The land afforded them and their children a multitude of opportunities if they were willing to work. Of course, they were. This optimistic spirit, and the confidence in the future that characterized the men and women who built America, is central to our national heritage.

Americans believe in progress, in the advancement of human civilization. This is the belief in a natural tendency for things to get better and better over time. Through the generations,

Americans have believed that their children would do better than they did, and they were proud and delighted when this came to pass. Some surveys indicate the recent economic downturn has shaken that belief, and politicians have sought to exploit the passing pessimism. When Jimmy Carter spoke of malaise in March 1980 (he never used that word, but his address to the nation was so dripping with pessimism that the *Boston Globe* editorialized that the speech was mere "Mush from the Wimp"), he went against the basic premise of America's founding. Carter's "malaise" speech contributed substantially to his defeat in that year's presidential election. As the sunny optimist, Ronald Reagan understood that it is always better to bet on the optimism and the energies of free Americans than against them.

The optimists create inventions, start new businesses, invest in and develop new technologies, write books, sing songs, build skyscrapers, and venture boldly "where no man has ever gone before." The optimists in America drive our entire society forward, inventing new medicines and technologies, solving problems, creating opportunities and jobs, and propelling America into the future. As Winston Churchill, half American (from his mother's side), put it, "A pessimist sees the difficulty in every opportunity; an optimist sees the opportunity in every difficulty."

Americans always seem to regard difficulties as opportunities. Recall the 2007 surge in Iraq. When many around the world—and even in the American Congress—thought the war was lost, President Bush tapped General David Petraeus to try a new approach. Both men were optimistic, and "perpetual optimism is a force multiplier," Colin Powell asserted. By the end of one year, fighting in Iraq had subsided. The surge worked, and the United States and Iraq enjoyed the benefits of a downturn in violence.

The Entrepreneurial Spirit

In times of economic difficulty, many look to government for solutions. But history has shown time and again that government lacks the ability to do much more than maintain the status quo. Often, government intervention makes matters worse. Just witness the American unemployment rate more than a year after an $800-plus billion "stimulus" package took effect. It was far higher than the Obama administration had predicted it would be if the government did nothing—a sobering lesson for all those who want Washington to prime the pump with tax-payer dollars. Americans knew that the stimulus was a bad idea, and the 27 percent disapproval of the bill shot up to 45 percent in less than one year.[1]

Individuals in the private sector will always be the key to economic success. The saying about "pulling yourself up by the bootstraps" typifies the optimistic spirit that, while not unique to America, is certainly American at its core. And America's entrepreneurs tend to be superoptimists. Especially for many entrepreneurs who start off at the bottom of the income ladder, this optimism is often justified. Research has found that by going into business for themselves, Americans who initially earn less than the median level of income (about $42,000 in 2008) will advance up the economic ladder significantly more quickly than those who work but do not go into business.[2]

Optimism can trump even the least promising personal circumstances. Consider the case of John Mackey, the CEO of Whole Foods Market. A University of Texas dropout, he and his girlfriend, Renee Lawson Hardy, borrowed $10,000 in 1978 and raised $35,000 more to found the first vegetarian super-market in Texas, which they called Safer Way. John and Renee ran their market on the first floor, operated a health food res-taurant on the second floor, and lived on the third floor. At that point in his life, John considered himself a democratic socialist, but that soon changed. He subsequently recalled:

> Operating a business was a real education for me. There were bills to pay and a payroll to be met and we had trouble doing either because we lost half of our $45,000 of capital in our first year. Our customers thought our prices were too high and our employees thought they were being underpaid. Renee and I were only being paid about $200 a month and the business was a real struggle. Nobody was very happy and Renee and I were now seen as capitalistic exploiters by our friends on the left. . . .
>
> I didn't think the charge of capitalist exploiters fit Renee and myself very well. In a nutshell, the economic system of democratic socialism was no longer intellectu-ally satisfying to me and I began to look around for more robust theories which would better explain business, eco-nomics, and society. Somehow or another I stumbled on to the works of Mises, Hayek, and Friedman, and had a complete revolution in my world view. The more I read, studied, and thought about economics and capitalism, the

more I came to realize that capitalism had been misunderstood and unfairly attacked by the left. In fact, democratic capitalism remains by far the best way to organize society to create prosperity, growth, freedom, self-actualization, and even equality.[3]

After two years, John and Renee merged Safer Way with a natural foods store and renamed the business Whole Foods. John went on to build Whole Foods into a national organization. Today, John Mackey is a major philanthropist, with a particular interest in animal welfare. His net worth is estimated at $1.8 billion.

The story of John Mackey proves what the American educator and Nobel Peace Prize laureate Nicholas Murray Butler said: "Optimism is the foundation of courage." Had he allowed his initial business difficulties to overwhelm him, or permitted his "friends on the left" to discourage him, there is no telling what he might be doing today, but it's a safe bet that he wouldn't have become the CEO of a national food chain.

The John Mackey story is one of the most remarkable success stories of our lifetime, but it is not the only one. Every single day Americans decide to act on their dreams, to reach for something someone has undoubtedly told them was "crazy" or "impossible." Not all will achieve it—that's just a simple fact of life—but many will, and the others will find their place and fulfillment elsewhere. The point is that regardless of their circumstances, they dared to try. As Norman Vincent Peale said, "Empty pockets never held anyone back. Only empty heads and hearts can do that."

Pessimism vs. Optimism

Although the clearly demonstrated path to any level of success is an optimistic disposition and a faith in your abilities, some people in our society take the opposite path. Instead of celebrating the most prosperous and exciting country in all human history, they see unfairness, poverty, injustice, oppression, discrimination, and racism everywhere. These people are pessimists.

The basic pessimist premise is that things are bad and getting worse. Pessimists reinforce this belief with the idea that people are not responsible for their problems, even when their problems are self-inflicted. For the pessimist with a malevolent worldview, there must always be an enemy of some kind lurking behind the curtain. There must always be someone to blame. If there is *a* wrong, someone must *be* wrong.

The pessimist only wants to demolish, never to build. The pessimist is destructive in his thinking, never constructive. The pessimist wants people who are not suffering to be punished. The pessimist is so preoccupied with getting even with those he believes are responsible for the problems he sees everywhere that he eventually forgets about helping the people he initially thought he was championing.

The pessimist in American society believes the reason some people are poor is that others are rich. He refuses to see any cause-and-effect relationship between behavior and result. This is the same as saying, "The reason some people are sick is that others are well."

Because they blame others for their problems, pessimists

seek solutions outside themselves for those problems. If you have no belief in yourself or your abilities, you'll have no faith in your capacity to solve your problems. A pessimist is always demanding help, regardless of whether that help is effective. Actress Shirley MacLaine once said, "Dwelling on the negative simply contributes to its power," and she was right.

In the 1960s President Lyndon Johnson declared a War on Poverty and unleashed the Great Society programs to end it. To date, more than $6 trillion has been spent in an attempt to rid the United States of poverty, yet poverty rates have stayed the same. Although the notion that government can solve the problem of poverty has been disproved not only in the United States but throughout Europe, this concept persists in the minds of many people. It seems that the one thing pessimists are optimistic about is that the failures of government will somehow correct themselves if they are allowed to continue indefinitely.

Humorist P. J. O'Rourke quipped, "You can't get rid of poverty by giving people money," and the federal government's attempt to do so proves it. But to really understand this failure, you must first clearly define the problem.

In 1978, economist Milton Friedman was asked if poverty was a market failure. He answered by wondering about how we define *poverty*: "While there are people in this country who are worse off than other people, by and large, even the poorest people in this country are relatively well off compared to the conditions in many other countries in the world. What we take as our standard of poverty is above the average income of all the people in the Soviet Union, let alone of the people in India or China or other countries." He went on to say, "Now that doesn't mean we should be satisfied with it. We are a wealthier country and we've been more productive, we should set higher standards by ourselves. But by the same token we ought to have a sense of proportion and we ought to recognize both the source and problem."[4]

Identifying a problem correctly is the only way we can address it effectively. The question of what constitutes poverty is constantly debated in this country. With the earned income tax credit (EITC) low-income workers are able to put extra money in their pockets. If the EITC were counted as income for the poverty calculation in 2008, the percentage of people in poverty would go from 14.0 percent to 12.7 percent. If we include government assistance of all kinds, the poverty rate would fall to 9.8 percent.[5] But the government doesn't count that money as income, so the poverty line remains higher than it, in fact, should be.

That is not to argue that there is no poverty in the United States or that it is not a problem that we, as a society, need to address. But a shotgun blast doesn't help when a scalpel is needed. Those in need of help are not receiving what they need when that help is diluted among others who don't need it.

So what is poverty, and how do the poor in the United States compare to the poor of the rest of the world? The average *poor person*, as defined by the government, has a living standard far higher than the public imagines. The following are facts about persons defined as *poor* by the Census Bureau, taken from various government reports:

- Forty-three percent of all poor households actually own homes. The average home owned by persons classified as poor has three bedrooms, one-and-a-half baths, a garage, and a porch or patio.

- Eighty percent of poor households have air-conditioning. By contrast, in 1970, only 36 percent of the entire US population enjoyed air-conditioning.

- Only 6 percent of poor households are overcrowded; 67 percent have more than two rooms per person.

- The typical poor American has more living space than the average individual living in Paris, London, Vienna, Athens, and other cities throughout Europe. (These comparisons are to average citizens in foreign countries, not to those classified as poor.)

- Nearly 75 percent of poor households own a car; 31 percent own two or more cars.

- Ninety-seven percent of poor households have a color television; more than 50 percent own two or more color televisions.

- Seventy-eight percent have a VCR or DVD player; 62 percent have cable or satellite TV reception.

- Eighty-nine percent own microwave ovens, more than 50 percent have a stereo, and more than 33 percent have an automatic dishwasher.

Overall, the typical American defined as poor by the government has a car, air-conditioning, a refrigerator, a stove, a clothes washer and dryer, and a microwave. He has two color televisions, cable or satellite TV reception, a VCR or DVD player, and a stereo. He is able to obtain medical care. His home is in good repair and is not overcrowded. By his own report, his family is not hungry, and he had sufficient funds in the past year to meet his family's essential needs. While this individual's life is not opulent, it is equally far from the popular images of dire poverty conveyed by the press, liberal activists, and "progressive" politicians.[6]

In sum, even Americans below the poverty line live lives that would have been considered comfortable just a few generations ago. The social safety net was supposed to be just that, a safety net, much like the net under a trapeze, designed to catch only the handful of people going through hard times and help them get back on their feet. Unfortunately it has turned into a fishing net, ensnaring generations in poverty.

In a 1978 interview with the *Times Herald*, Milton Friedman described that era's welfare system this way:

> There is only one word to describe the welfare situation and that's one of our famous four-letter-words: mess! The so-called welfare program is a collection of a large number of separate programs in which most of the money that is spent does not go to the people whom you would like to get it. The major beneficiaries are intermediaries—the bureaucrats who administer it, the agencies or organizations that benefit from it—and that is also the major obstacle to reform.[7]

After two of his vetoes, President Clinton finally signed meaningful welfare reform in 1996. For the first time, welfare recipients were required to find work and had a time limit on how long they could receive benefits. This move caused a panic among the professional pessimists since the cornerstone of their power base was firmly set in the dependent class. Doom and gloom were foreseen.

At the time, for example, the Children's Defense Fund said the welfare reform law would increase "child poverty nationwide by 12% . . . make children hungrier . . . [and] reduce the incomes of one-fifth of all families with children in the nation." It further declared the new reform law an "outrage . . . that will hurt and impoverish millions of American children." The reform "will leave a moral blot on [Clinton's] presidency and on our nation that will never be forgotten."

Yet, predictably, the reforms worked. The number of children living in poverty dropped from 14.6 million in 1995 to 11.7 million in 2001. Overall, by 2001 US Census data showed that 3.5 million fewer people were living in poverty thanks to the new law. The "moral blot" turned out to become President Clinton's most lasting policy legacy.

The new law, in many ways, was effective in instilling optimism in many people who had never had it. Once a person, after a lifetime of dependency, gets a taste of independence, optimism grows naturally.

Much more needs to be done, and there will always be horror stories that professional pessimists can find and present as if they were the norm. But statistics demonstrate the success of welfare reform. As the late New York senator Daniel Patrick Moynihan (himself a staunch opponent of the 1996 reforms) said, "Everyone is entitled to his own opinion, but not his own facts."

Optimism is the fuel that feeds our dreams. It provides us with the hope necessary to innovate, invent, and aspire, and the willingness to take the risks essential to achieve. Robbed of optimism, people will languish and wallow in self-pity. Their lives, and the lives of their children, will stagnate. While not everyone can reach the level of success of a John Mackey, everyone can aspire and achieve things that will improve their lot in life and aid their children so they can do better still—provided that the government stays out of the way.

The Welfare State

Unfortunately government rarely stays out of the way, and its efforts to improve matters often backfire. The social welfare state in Europe has stifled innovation and aspiration. Why work hard to improve your lot in life when the government will provide you with enough to get by and punish you through an oppressive tax and regulatory system if you do more than get by?

In the United States we have drifted perilously close to a similar situation, with almost half of Americans not paying any income taxes. These folks have no incentive to limit the growth of government since they're not paying for it. They also have no interest in recognizing that when the government punishes success, our entire economy suffers.

In 1983, a brilliant French intellectual named Jean-François Revel wrote the widely discussed book *How Democracies Perish*. "Democracy," he wrote, "tends to ignore, even deny, threats to its existence because it loathes doing what is necessary to counter them." Hence, Revel predicted, the totalitarian Soviet bloc would triumph over the democratic West.[8]

As we all know, Revel's pessimism proved unwarranted; optimistic Western leaders like Ronald Reagan and Margaret Thatcher knew exactly how to counter the Soviet threat. But another pessimistic intellectual, the eighteenth-century Scottish historian Alexander Tytler, may yet turn out to have been a truer prophet than Revel. "A democracy cannot exist as a permanent form of government," Tytler is supposed to have said. "It can only exist until the majority discovers it can vote itself largess out of the public treasury. After that, the majority always votes for the candidate promising the most benefits with the result the democracy collapses because of the loose fiscal policy ensuing, always to be followed by a dictatorship, then a monarchy."[9]

We are not there yet. The bad news, however, is that in 2009, 64.3 million Americans depended on the government for their daily housing, food, and health care. As the number of Americans who believe themselves entitled to free government benefits continues to rise, the very survival of our form of government is called into question. William Beach, who directs Heritage's Center for Data Analysis and has been tracking Americans' growing dependence on government since 1962, believes that our republican form of government can probably withstand some "very limited increases" in the dependent population. But over the next twenty-five years, more than *seventy-seven million* boomers will begin collecting Social Security checks, drawing Medicare benefits, and relying on long-term care under Medicaid. This tsunami of increased dependency is likely to overwhelm our political system:

Can [our institutions] stand against the swelling ranks of Americans who believe themselves entitled to government benefits for which they pay few or no taxes? Are Americans completely indifferent to history's many examples of experiments in republican government collapsing under the weight of just such a population? Are Americans near a tipping point in the nature of their government and the principles that tie it to civil life? A fair reading of the trends and the data . . . leads almost inescapably to the conclusion that, yes, Americans have reached that point.[10]

We fervently hope that Alexander Tytler's pessimistic forecast about the inevitable collapse of all democracies—backed up by the alarming data compiled by Bill Beach—proves no more accurate than Jean-François Revel's gloomy prophecy. But we mustn't fool ourselves: the hour is late, and our situation is grim. New Jersey's governor, Chris Christie, has observed:

We are teetering on the edge of disaster. And I love when people talk about American exceptionalism. But American exceptionalism has to include the courage to do the right thing. It cannot just be a belief that because we're exceptional everything will work out OK. Part of truly being exceptional is being willing to do the difficult things, to stop playing the political games, stop looking at the bumper pool of politics, and to step up and start doing the right thing.[11]

For our elected representatives, doing the right thing today means telling the American people that America's future is in jeopardy and that painful sacrifices must be made. Far from punishing politicians who "tell it like is," Americans will welcome honest accounting and straight talk. After all, we are not a nation of timid sheep in need of a Big Government shepherd, but descendants of proud and brave immigrants and pioneers. Optimistic leaders who place their bets on the toughness and resilience of the American Spirit always come out ahead.

CHAPTER 6

Foresight

Go to the ant, O sluggard,
Observe her ways and be wise. . . .
The ants are not a strong people,
But they prepare their food in the summer.

—Proverbs 6:6; 30:25 NASB

Preparing for Tomorrow

We live in the now. The current moment is all we have, but the future will come whether we're ready for it or not. Foresight helps to ensure that we have the best now possible when it gets here. Thinking long term is not only the smart thing to do; it's a necessary component for success, be it in our personal lives or in the life of our country.

Personal Foresight

The idea of saving for a rainy day is a common one, but one that is sometimes difficult to achieve. In our personal lives it is important to prepare for the unexpected. General George S. Patton once said, "A good plan today is better than a perfect plan tomorrow." The impossibility of knowing the future can be combated only by sensible planning. "Hope for the best, prepare for the worst," the old saying goes.

In times of prosperity, it's natural for people to get swept up in the moment and spend as though the good times will never end. But in the back of our minds we all know nothing lasts forever. Living beyond our means is a constant temptation, especially with the ease of credit cards at our disposal. But it is important to remember the volatility of life and to plan for the inevitable rainy day.

Today, personal savings rates are beginning to rise, albeit slowly. In the early to mid-1990s, Americans had a savings rate of 7 to 8 percent, but that started to steadily decline until, in the mid-2000s, it dipped below 1 percent. Thankfully that trend is reversing, and saving rates have risen to about 4 percent.

This is an encouraging trend, especially after years of living beyond our means as individuals. The housing bubble started inflating in the late 1990s and popped in 2007–8. Fueled by people purchasing more home than they could afford and banks willing to lend money to nearly anyone, regardless of their ability to repay the money, this personal debt *Titanic* hit the iceberg and started to sink the economy. Once the hangover of subprime housing boom subsides completely, people will be well advised to continue saving more of their income and return to the responsible borrowing that has been a staple of American life.

Professional Foresight

Successful people seem to have a long-term vision combined with a short-term focus. Their future goals, defined clearly, determine and shape their present actions. They take the time to be clear about what they want and about the steps they will have to take in order to get it. They begin taking these steps, one at a time, month after month, and year after year, until they finally arrive at their destination. Thomas Edison explained, "Good fortune is what happens when opportunity meets with planning."

Foresight is closely associated with success and advancement in America. After years of research, Professor Edward Banfield of Harvard University concluded that the key to upward social and economic mobility in America is long-term perspective. People who succeed greatly in life seem to be those who project forward ten and twenty years in planning their daily actions. The most respected and esteemed men and women in our society are clearly long-term thinkers. After all, "if you don't know where you're going, you'll end up someplace else," Yogi Berra declared.

For example, in every survey of the most admired professions in America, doctors come out at the top. Everyone knows a doctor must work hard throughout extra years of schooling and then dedicate years to medical study, internship, residency, and practice before being fully qualified to practice medicine.

Doctors made enormous sacrifices in the early years of their lives, often emerging into their thirties deep in debt, in order to be able to practice medicine for the rest of their careers.

Perhaps the most important word in long-term success is *sacrifice*. Every great achievement requires enormous sacrifice in terms of time, money, effort (both physical and mental), and financial pain before the goal is achieved. This is true in every field. Even people who achieve success in show business and the arts have usually worked for many thousands of hours to develop their skills and credentials. Highly accomplished people in any walk of life have usually dedicated many years of hard work and sacrifice before they have become successful. "The secret to success is constancy of purpose," Benjamin Franklin said.

The American Dream is open to all, but it is only realized by those willing to work hard and pay the price of success, in advance, for many years. The contest is always between the competing ideas of short-term pain for long-term gain and short-term gain for long-term pain.

H. L. Hunt, at one time the richest self-made American, was asked the secret of success. He replied, "There are only two things necessary for success in America. First, decide exactly what you want. Most people never do this, which is why they achieve very little. Second, determine the price that you are going to have to pay to get what you want, and get busy paying that price. If you do these two things, your future is virtually unlimited."

In the 1950s a milkshake mixer salesman had fallen on hard times, sales were down, and he was losing customers. The man was in his late forties and wondering what to do next. One day he got an order for eight machines from a restaurant in San

Bernardino, California. The size of the order confused and intrigued him, so he left his Illinois home to visit the customer.

The owners, brothers named Dick and Mac, ran a small burger joint that was unlike anything the salesman had ever seen. They sold only hamburgers and cheeseburgers, fries, shakes, and other beverages. Most interesting to the salesman was the assembly line system they had for food preparation, which allowed the small restaurant to serve a lot of people quickly. The salesman saw potential, but the brothers were not interested in opening more locations. A deal was struck between the salesman, named Ray Kroc, and the brothers, Dick and Mac McDonald, to allow Ray the exclusive rights to their method and their name. In 1955 McDonald's was born.

Ray was ambitious; the McDonald brothers were not. Ray had a plan; the McDonald brothers did not. In 1961 Ray paid the brothers $2.7 million for complete ownership of McDonald's. Ray had a plan to open one thousand locations, putting a McDonald's within a short drive of every American. His success was something for which even he couldn't have planned. Two years later Ray had his five hundredth location, and in 1968 he opened his one thousandth.

Ray Kroc's vision for McDonald's was clear and effective. His owner's manual for franchisees contained very specific information on how to do business, from how much a burger should weigh to how much mustard and ketchup should be used. His plan to provide good food at a low price to people in their neighborhoods and a familiar oasis for travelers turned into the most successful restaurant chain in the world. Currently McDonald's has more than twenty-five thousand locations around the globe.

Not every endeavor can turn into a billion-dollar industry, but any successful endeavor, be it professional or personal, can learn from the success of others. Dreaming is one thing; planning is another. A dream is about an idea; planning is about how to implement the idea and how to make it a reality. The old adage "If you fail to plan, you plan to fail" is true.

Government Foresight

As important as foresight is in personal and professional settings, it is doubly important when it comes to government. And one of the greatest examples of foresight in the history of the world is the American founding. It was meant to inaugurate a *novus ordo seclorum* (a new order for the ages), and it has. Perhaps the main reason why it continues to inspire men and women of every race, religion, and walk of life is that it rests on principles that are true not just for its own time, but *for all time*. President Calvin Coolidge made this point with great clarity in 1926 on the 150th anniversary of the Declaration of Independence:

> About the Declaration there is a finality that is exceedingly restful. It is often asserted that the world has made a great deal of progress since 1776, that we have had new thoughts and new experiences which have given us a great advance over the people of that day, and that we may therefore very well discard their conclusions for something more modern. But that reasoning can not be applied to this great charter. If all men are created equal, that is final. If they are endowed

with inalienable rights, that is final. No advance, no progress can be made beyond these propositions. If anyone wishes to deny their truth or their soundness, the only direction in which he can proceed historically is not forward, but backward toward the time when there was no equality, no rights of the individual, no rule of the people. Those who wish to proceed in that direction can not lay claim to progress. They are reactionary. Their ideas are not more modern, but more ancient, than those of the Revolutionary fathers.[1]

When we assert that America's founding principles are true for all time, we don't mean to suggest that Americans should return to earlier, simpler days. As Heritage scholar Matthew Spalding has written,

Renewing America's principles doesn't mean going back to the eighteenth century, or some other time for that matter. Think of principles as the unchanging standards that inform changing experiences. The question is not, "What Would the Founders Do?" but what will we do as we go forward toward an unknowable future with these fixed principles as our trustworthy guides. It is not about looking *back* to the past, but rather looking *down* at our roots in order to look *up* to our highest ideals.[2]

In the twentieth century, the American statesman who best exemplified the conservative ideal of looking back to our roots in order to shape our future was Ronald Reagan. Unlike virtually every other American politician of his day, Reagan strongly believed that we could win the Cold War, and this belief rested on his faith in the American system, his conviction that the principles on which America is founded are true, while those on which the Soviet Union rested were false. Heritage scholar Joseph Shattan wrote about Reagan:

> The reason Reagan differed from virtually every other American political figure was that he had boundless faith in the strength of the free enterprise system and boundless contempt for Soviet collectivism. Whereas other politicians viewed the Cold Was as a complex struggle between two more or less evenly matched superpowers, Reagan saw it as a totally uneven contest between two *systems*, one of which (capitalism) was infinitely superior, both morally and economically, to the other. It seemed self-evident to him that the United States would win the Cold War, provided that its economy was freed from the shackles of big government and allowed to reach its full potential. Hence, promoting America's economic recovery through tax cuts and deregulation became, for Reagan, the basis for any winning Cold War strategy.[3]

While the rest of the world was content to play nice with the Soviet Union, Reagan believed that Soviet communism was on its last legs and that this gave the United States the opportunity to administer the coup de grace by challenging the Soviets on a host of economic, military, political, and technological fronts. His strategy was vindicated when the Berlin Wall fell in 1989 and when the Soviet Union was dissolved in 1991. Shattan noted,

One can cite all sorts of secondary reasons—the strength of the American economy, the weakness of the Soviet system, the astuteness of Reagan's foreign policy advisers, the blunders of Gorbachev and his team—to explain Reagan's achievement; but the primary reason was that Ronald Reagan had a profound (his critics would say childlike or simplistic) faith in freedom. . . . He simply *knew* that there was no way a closed society could defeat an open society once the open society made up its mind to prevail. The rest is commentary.[4]

Unfortunately government rarely engages in the kind of principled and bold acts of foresight that characterized the Reagan administration's approach to the Cold War. Nowhere is this more evident than in our current unsustainable spending spree. The Obama administration has used the recession as an excuse for an unprecedented expansion of government spending and deficits. Only at the height of World War II has Washington matched current levels of spending (25 percent of gross domestic product) and deficits (10 percent of gross domestic product). By 2020, *interest* spending on the national debt will triple to approximately $600 billion annually—more than Congress spends on education, energy, transportation, housing, and environmental protection combined. And even when the recession ends, runaway spending is expected to keep annual budget deficits over $1 trillion, which could result in sharply higher interest rates, painful tax increases, and even a Greece-like economic crisis.

Beyond its economic consequences, however, runaway government spending and deficits pose a moral challenge: it is simply *wrong* to shackle our children and grandchildren with disabling debt and heavy taxes. Yet that is exactly what we have done:

> Washington's reckless spending spree of the past several years and unwillingness to confront the mountains of debt coming soon from unreformed federal entitlement programs threaten the economic and social future of the generation currently between the ages of 5 and 30. The 115 million Americans in this Debt-Paying Generation could experience enormous adverse effects from having to pay down the greatest debt in world history. Indeed, the people in the Debt-Paying Generation could end their working lives as the least improved generation relative to the one that preceded them in U.S. history. They will marry later, have fewer children, poorer health, and lower incomes because they must pay the trillions of debt from excessive spending today and from the tsunami of debt coming from unfunded liabilities in Medicare, Social Security, and Medicaid.[5]

Reining in Runaway Spending and Deficits

Saying government spending has gotten out of control is an understatement on the scale of saying Michael Jordan was just a good basketball player or Babe Ruth hit some home runs. Thanks to unbridled spending, corporate bailouts, and the takeover of the best health-care system in the world, America stands on the verge of a financial cliff that endangers our future, our children's future, and our grandchildren's future.

In *Solutions for America*, a comprehensive guide for governing published in the summer of 2010, the Heritage Foundation laid out a series of reforms that must be adopted if we are to avoid fiscal catastrophe:

- **Enact spending caps.** Washington has no enforceable limits on its spending. As long as Congress remains under pressure to spend, members need annual spending caps to help them set priorities and make the necessary trade-offs. Congress should enact a firm cap on the annual increase in total government spending, limited to inflation plus population growth. It should also include triggers and other protections to prevent lawmakers from bypassing this cap.
- **Stop digging.** A recession is no excuse for irresponsible federal spending. Washington should repeal the remaining stimulus funds, which have failed to create jobs and growth. Any new unemployment assistance should be offset by spending cuts elsewhere. *Most important, lawmakers must repeal ObamaCare, a ticking spending and deficit time bomb.*
- **Rein in entitlements.** Social Security, Medicare, and Medicaid are driving long-term deficit growth. It is impossible to rein in runaway spending significantly without fundamentally reforming these programs.
- **Empower states.** Washington taxes families, subtracts a hefty administrative cost, and sends the remaining revenues back to state and local governments with specific rules dictating how to spend the money. Instead of performing many functions poorly, Congress should fo-

cus on performing a few functions well. Most highway, education, justice, and economic development programs should be devolved to state and local governments, which have the flexibility to tailor local programs to local needs.

- **Empower the private sector.** Anyone who has dealt with the post office or lived in public housing knows how wasteful, inefficient, and unresponsive government can be. Government ownership of business also crowds out private companies and encourages protected entities to take unnecessary risks. After promising profits, government-owned businesses frequently lose billions of dollars, leaving taxpayers to foot the bill. Any government function that can be found in the yellow pages should be a candidate for privatization.

- **Ban corporate welfare.** Even before the financial bailouts, Washington spent more on corporate welfare ($90 billion) than on homeland security ($70 billion). Americans should not be taxed to subsidize profitable companies. Lawmakers could start by reforming America's largest corporate welfare program—farm subsidies, which are overwhelmingly distributed to large, profitable agribusinesses rather than struggling family farmers. Other programs, like the Technology Innovation Program (formerly known as Advanced Technology Program), should be eliminated.

- **Eliminate pork and waste.** Each year, Washington loses $98 billion to payment errors and pays $25 billion to maintain vacant federal properties. Washington also diverts about $20 billion annually into pork projects, corrupting the legislative process by assigning taxpayer dollars on the basis of lobbying rather than merit.

- **Bring federal pay in line with the private sector.** Besides doing too many things best left to the private sector and the states, the federal government pays its employees substantially more than they would earn in the private sector. Total compensation—hourly wages plus benefits—is 30 to 40 percent above that of comparable private sector workers. Aligning federal compensation with market rates would save taxpayers about $47 billion annually.[6]

Without serious planning for the future, America's future will be grim. The recent unrest in Europe, from Greece to Great Britain, is a warning, a crystal ball through which we can see what might well happen to us should we succumb to the temptations of irresponsible government.

Foresight Means Sacrifice

Foresight is a difficult virtue to embrace, especially for aging baby boomers now entering the age of retirement. Former Heritage scholar Chuck Donovan, a baby boomer, has written:

The people of the Greatest Generation viewed their kids as their crowning achievement. But too many of us did not inherit their greatest virtue: an ability to sacrifice. Instead we embraced instant gratification and self-infatuation. We arrogantly thought we had invented sex, when all we did was invent new ways to trivialize it. We mistook wants for needs, borrowed too much, saved too little. In the process we helped our proud and productive nation recast itself as a consumption-dependent economy. Ours became the Age of Appetites.

Appetites have consequences. Out-of-wedlock births are up more than 600% since the 1960s. Household debt is soaring. Our sense of middle-class entitlement is soaring, too.

We boomers have run the race poorly, but we can finish strong. We enter our last laps with difficult decisions before us. We can demand flush retirements and lavish health care, board gaudy cruise ships, and foist today's deficits on the next generation. Or we can relearn the meaning of sacrifice and the virtues that gave us birth. Though the hour is late, the choice is ours to make.[7]

We, as a nation, must act now to correct the course of our ship of state before it's too late. Having the foresight to address America's deficit and debt problems *today*, before they grow totally unmanageable, is the only way to ensure that the American Spirit lives on in future generations.

CHAPTER 7

Good Citizenship

Every good citizen makes his country's honor his own, and cherishes it not only as precious but as sacred. He is willing to risk his life in its defense and is conscious that he gains protection while he gives it.

—Andrew Jackson

Citizenship is what makes a republic; monarchies can get along without it.

—Mark Twain

The first requisite of a good citizen in this republic of ours is that he shall be able and willing to pull his own weight.

—Theodore Roosevelt

Good Citizenship

Merriam-Webster's online dictionary defines *citizenship* this way:

1: the status of being a citizen

2a: membership in a community (as a college) b : the quality of an individual's response to membership in a community

Citizenship, the first definition, is achieved by birth or action. In the United States we make no distinction between natural-born citizens and those naturalized, with the exception of the constitutional requirement that the president be a natural-born citizen. All the rights and protections of citizenship are afforded without prejudice or qualifications. But citizenship and good citizenship, the second definition, are different matters entirely; one is granted, the other earned.

Country as Community

America has always been a melting pot. We are a nation founded by people from all over the world who came here seeking a better life for themselves and their families. Individuals have found success in the United States through assimilation while simultaneously maintaining their heritage. The strength of the United States lies in the people of the United States acting in ways that benefit us as individuals and, by extension, our communities.

This is not to say that we, as a people, cannot come together as one when circumstances warrant. After the atrocities of

September 11, 2001, the nation was united, as it is after every tragedy. That was our strength against the Soviet Union, and it is our strength today in our struggle against radical Islamo-fascists.

Our national motto, *E Pluribus Unum*, became a reality after December 7, 1941, when the empire of Japan attacked Pearl Harbor. Upon hearing the news of the first attack on the United States since the British invasion in the War of 1812, our nation of individuals united as one against Japan and its allies, Germany and Italy. In the months following the attack, America's military personnel grew from 1.933 million in October 1941 to 3 million by April 1942, and 5.2 million by October 1942. By October 1944 it would contain 11.9 million personnel who had signed up to serve. Those soldiers, the vast majority of whom had never set foot on the islands of Hawaii or known any of the 2,340 men killed in the attack, were not directly affected or threatened by the Japanese assault, yet they signed up to protect their fellow citizens and nation. The patriotism of these men and women, their sense of community, and courage—their Americanism, if you will—brought them together to volunteer to risk their lives in ways they could hardly foresee. An attack on one was an attack on all.

This sense of community was necessary for our freedom and liberty to survive. Rightly called "the Greatest Generation," America's World War II soldiers fought the "axis of evil" of their day and won. When they came home, they were duly celebrated, then they went back to their individual lives. The bonds they formed were between individuals, brothers-in-arms. It was a bond only people who have been through something like war can experience. That sense of brotherhood was necessary for them to survive the horrors they encountered. When they returned, they were changed as individuals, but they did not seek to impose the conformity and discipline of military life onto their civilian communities.

While women served bravely in the military too, on the home front they also proved that they were good citizens. The war effort needed an endless stream of equipment, and there was a shortage of men for the factories that built the equipment. Women joined the workforce and performed jobs they had never done before. These were jobs requiring skills many believed that women lacked. While some women were undoubtedly uncomfortable stepping outside their world as they had known it, they were urgently needed, and their sense of duty drove them to do what needed to be done. The war could not have been won without the sense of community and responsibility that emerges spontaneously whenever America is attacked.

The Color-Blind Society

Good citizenship requires adherence to the golden rule, "Do unto others as you would have them do unto you." Without that two-way street unnatural inequities become entrenched, and societal cancers can grow. We, as a nation, learned this lesson the hard way.

When our nation was founded, accepting the evil of slavery was necessary for unity to win our fight against the British and to form a cohesive national government. Slave states would not have joined the fight or the Union, were it not for this horrible bargain. Without it, the Revolutionary War could not have been won, and our nation would never have come into being.

For more than eighty years, slavery was an open wound on our national body. The Civil War put an end to the practice but not the mentality. Jim Crow laws were the new evil that replaced slavery for a century, oppressing blacks and other minorities.

In the 1960s those wounds were cauterized with the passage of the Civil Rights Act, and the scars left behind have been fading ever since. America has moved much closer to the "more perfect Union" for which our Founding Fathers hoped.

Despite the occasional hateful act—always roundly and publicly condemned—that endures like the last remnants of lint in former pockets of racism, we have evolved into the nation Rev. Martin Luther King Jr. spoke of in his immortal "I Have a Dream" speech: "I have a dream that my four little children will one day live in a nation where they will not be judged by the color of their skin but by the content of their character."

Although it is impossible to remove all vestiges of irrational hatred based on race, ethnicity, or national origin from all individuals, as a society we are more color-blind than any other in history. Having gone from slavery, "Irish need not apply," and Japanese internment camps to where we are today, we are fulfilling the truths that our Founding Fathers held as self-evident in the Declaration of Independence: "That all Men are created equal, that they are endowed by their Creator with certain unalienable Rights, that among these are Life, Liberty, and the Pursuit of Happiness."

Good Citizenship at the Local Level

Not every act of citizenship requires a grand gesture or sacrifice; every small, simple action adds an important thread to the fabric of a community. Everything from helping a neighbor carry in her groceries to holding the door open for someone to voting in a local election or participating in a block party makes you an active member of a community. These actions are not mandatory, but every act of simple kindness adds a sense of belonging that breeds further acts of kindness and strengthens the community.

One simple act of inspired compassionate good citizenship took place in the spring of 2010 in Indianapolis. The Roncalli High School girls' junior varsity softball team, which had not lost a game in two and a half years, was taking on Marshall, playing their first-ever game. To say the Marshall players were outmatched would be an understatement. Marshall showed up to the game with only two bats, no helmets, eleven girls who had never played a game, and a coach who had never seen one. The players did not know where to stand in the batter's box or even which base was first.

After an inning and a half, and nine walks by Marshall pitchers, everything was in place for a Roncalli slaughter. But something funny happened on the way to humiliation—Marshall won!

They did not score more runs than the Roncalli powerhouse; they won by forfeit. The players and coach of Roncalli decided that humiliating Marshall was not something they wanted to do. They would rather spend their time together on the field teaching Marshall how to play the game, and that was exactly what happened.

The girls from Roncalli spent the next two hours teaching their opponents the fundamentals of softball. Roncalli coach Jeff Traylor described the scene after the forfeit in a letter. When the girls from Roncalli came over, they

> introduced themselves and with the Holy Spirit active in their hearts took the field with the Marshall girls to show them positions, how to field a ground ball, how to throw, how to catch, where to stand, what an out was. The pitchers from Roncalli worked with the pitchers from Marshall showing them technique and release points. Our coaches were teaching their coaches how to soft toss and different drills they can use.
>
> After about 20–30 minutes each Roncalli Girl matched up one on one with the Marshall Players and taught them how to hit. I will forever remember the image of 11 sets of players spread out in our outfield soft tossing and hitting off tees, one at a time the Marshall girls would come in to hit off of the pitchers and one at a time I could see determination and a desire to just be better. As they hit the ball their faces LIT UP! They were high-fiving and hugging the girls from Roncalli, thanking them for teaching to them the game.
>
> Almost as emotional was the look of pure love on the faces of the Roncalli girls. I knew that one wrong attitude, one babying approach from our players would shut down the Marshall team who already were down for thinking they were quitters but our girls made me as proud as I have ever been to be a Rebel because they knew they could do something small to make a large difference!

That sense of pride, that sense of community, is the good citizenship that will positively impact the lives of everyone on the field that day. Through a simple act of sportsmanship, the girls from Roncalli started a ripple effect that will be felt well beyond their immediate surroundings and inspire similar acts throughout the country.

Contemporary Americans are the heirs of a long and proud tradition of good citizenship. As the distinguished French visitor Alexis de Tocqueville observed nearly 180 years ago:

> I have often seen Americans make great and real sacrifices to the public welfare; and I have noticed a hundred instances in which they hardly ever failed to lend faithful support to one another. The free institutions which the inhabitants of the United States possess, and the political rights of which they make so much use, remind every citizen, and in a thousand ways, that he lives in society. They every instant impress upon his mind the notion that it is the duty as well as the interest of men to make themselves useful to their fellow creatures; and as he sees no particular ground of animosity to them, since he is never either their master or their slave, his heart readily leans to the side of kindness.[1]

We are individuals with no legal obligation to act on behalf of or in the interest of anyone else, yet we do. Random acts of kindness, of sportsmanship, of bravery are all integral parts of a community. And a successful community is a voluntary community whose members, as Tocqueville said, are neither masters nor slaves, and in which citizens act unselfishly to help one another.

The Tea Party Movement

In recent years, however, America's traditional sense of community has begun to fracture. Former US Court of Appeals judge Robert H. Bork observed, "Radical individualism, radical egalitarianism, omnipresent and omni-competent government, the politicization of the culture, and the battle for advantages through politics shatter a society into fragments of isolated individuals and angry groups. Social peace and cohesion decline as loneliness and alienation rise."[2]

But American society is not doomed to break apart into thousands of angry, isolated, and mutually hostile fragments. Powerful forces have risen up to contain and reverse the ravages of modern liberalism and restore a sense of community. One of the most encouraging of these countervailing forces is the Tea Party movement.

The Tea Party movement is a good example of a spontaneous, voluntary community. Millions of Americans, acting individually, have come together to defend the American Spirit that they (correctly) feel is under siege. As two astute students of the movement, Scott Rasmussen and Douglas Schoen, have noted, Tea Party members feel that "we are no longer living in the country we once knew. A country where everyone has the opportunity to thrive and succeed. Where hard work equals opportunity. Where the powerful submit to the people. Where democracy reigns. Where those who play by the rules are rewarded with a better life for themselves and their families."[3]

Tea Party members are especially disappointed with their elected representatives in Washington who, they (correctly) feel, have become a "ruling class" of sorts, removed from, and indifferent to, the concerns of the people who elected them. Rasmussen and Schoen pointed out that "the gap [between] Americans who want to govern themselves and the politicians who want to rule over them may be as big today as between the colonies and England during the 18th century."[4]

To revive the American Spirit, the Tea Party movement is calling for a return to first principles. Like the civil rights movement of the 1950s and '60s, the Tea Party movement draws its inspiration from America's founding and seeks to renew and restore the "self-evident" truths of the Declaration. That is why the Heritage Foundation honored the Tea Party movement with its Salvatori Prize for American Citizenship in 2010.

In presenting the Salvatori Prize, the director of Heritage's Simon Center for American Studies, Matthew Spalding, recounted the story of Levi Preston, a young man who fought in the opening engagement of the American Revolution, the April 19, 1775, Battle of Concord. He was asked years later why he went out to fight that day against the best-trained and best-armed military force in the world. Was it the intolerable oppressions of the British? "No." The Stamp Act? "No." The tax on tea? "No." The philosophical works of Herrington, Sidney, and Locke? "Never heard of them." And then Levi Preston explained his real motive for fighting the British: "You see, we had always governed ourselves, we always intended to govern ourselves, and they didn't mean that we should."

Having deftly drawn his audience into the past, Spalding proceeded to make the all-important connection between then and now:

Someday in the future, some historian will ask some individual, perhaps one of you, "Why did you get involved in the Tea Parties? Was it the spending? Was it the bailouts? Was it health care?" "No," they will answer. "It was very simple. We had always governed ourselves, we had always intended to govern ourselves, and those liberals didn't think that we should."[5]

Of course, three hundred million Americans cannot *literally* govern themselves. The Polish-born scholar and philosopher Leszek Kolakowski pointed out:

> Apart from anything else, it would not be technically feasible. There can only be certain safeguards whereby the people can keep an eye on what the government is doing and replace it with another if it so chooses. . . . The means by which a people exercises control over its government are never perfect, but the most effective way mankind has so far invented to avoid tyranny is precisely to go on strengthening the instruments of social control over governments and restricting the range of government powers to the bare minimum necessary to maintain social order: the regulation of all areas of our lives, after all, is what totalitarian power is all about.[6]

Unfortunately even in a system of representative self-government such as ours, government leaders who enjoy a substantial amount of power for a prolonged time often come to feel entitled to it and to regard ordinary citizens as somehow inferior. That is why, when asked to define the best leader, the Athenian philosopher Socrates replied, "The man who steps forward in time of need—motivated not by ego or financial gain but by a sense of duty to benefit the society to which he belongs—then, when the task is completed, returns to his former life, no wealthier than when he began."[7]

The Tea Party movement appears to be producing the kinds of leaders that Socrates most admired: men and women motivated not by a desire for glory or gain, but by a sense of duty to their country at a critical moment in its history. The final word on the Tea Party's impact has yet to be written. Whether its leaders retain their idealism and determination to make government smaller, less intrusive, and more responsive to the electorate—or whether they eventually become part of the very "ruling class" they have pledged to overthrow—is one of the most crucial questions facing America today. The answer may well determine the fate of the American Spirit.

CHAPTER 8

Honesty

Honesty is the first chapter in the book of wisdom.

—Thomas Jefferson

The trite saying that honesty is the best policy has met with the just criticism that honesty is not policy. The real honest man is honest from conviction of what is right, not from policy.

—Robert E. Lee

All men profess honesty as long as they can. To believe all men honest would be folly. To believe none so is something worse.

—John Quincy Adams

The Value of Honesty

Of all the traits a person can possess, honesty is the most important. Without honesty every other trait is diminished, some to the point of irrelevance. What good is seeking the advice of a wise man if that man's honesty is in doubt? How can you go into business with a partner you can't trust? Why should you sacrifice for your country if your leaders regularly lie to you? In personal, business, and governmental relations, a lack of honesty can destroy any progress made or hopes for the future. Thomas Paine wrote, "Of more worth is one honest man to society, and in the eyes of God, than all the crowned ruffians that ever lived."

The history of the United States is replete with stories and fables celebrating the honesty of our national heroes. "Honest" Abe Lincoln and the story of George Washington and the cherry tree are but two of the best-known examples.

The virtue of honesty is reinforced by a feeling of self-respect. True honesty is impossible without a sense of self-respect that can be gained only through one's actions. Every person is capable of discerning right from wrong; the honest American not only knows what's right but also does what's right.

Clarence Thomas, associate justice of the United States Supreme Court, exemplifies the American virtue of honesty in his rise from poverty to one of the most powerful positions in the country. He attributes his strong sense of right and wrong to the example set by his grandparents. "As hard as I try," he told a Heritage audience,

I cannot discuss the issue of character, or much that is of lasting importance to me, without referring to the two great heroes of my life: my grandparents. They were honest, hard-working people who lived a simple, honest life with clear rules. . . . They were temperate in their drinking, modest in their dress, frugal in their spending. As someone from my generation might have said some years ago, "They talked the talk and walked the walk." They focused on what they could do—the seemingly small things that in the short term maintained order, but in the long term built character.[1]

The lessons that Thomas learned in his grandparents' home served him well in later life. When he was a young attorney in Missouri, working for little more than $500 a month and struggling to pay his bills, he found a wallet on his way to work one day that contained more than $600. At first he thought "it was a gift from Heaven." After taxes and bills he lived off an average of $10 a month, and this $600 find would surely make the next few months considerably easier on him. But after a few moments of temptation, he knew the right thing to do.

The wallet's owner, a brusque elderly man who seemed not at all thankful for Thomas's honesty, took his wallet back and offered Thomas a five-dollar bill in return. Thomas refused to accept the money and said that he hoped the man would return someone else's wallet if the situation were reversed. In his book *My Grandfather's Son*, Thomas noted the role that honesty played on this occasion and its effect on his life:

I learned two lessons that morning. The first one was that honesty is what you do when no one is looking. The second one was more important, so much so that I came to think of it as a defining moment in my ethical development: my needs, however great they might be, didn't convert wrong to right or bad to good. That man's wallet wasn't mine, no matter how much I needed the money, or how rude he happened to be. I often had occasion to remind myself in years to come that self-interest isn't a principle—it's just self-interest.[2]

Public Honesty

Nowadays, it often seems that the public sector suffers from an honesty deficit. Comedians regularly point to examples of political dishonesty, as do politicians (some with honesty problems of their own). Actually it has always been this way. The journalist and critic H. L. Mencken jokingly expressed Americans' longstanding mistrust of politicians when he said, "It is inaccurate to say that I hate everything. I am strongly in favor of common sense, common honesty, and common decency. This makes me forever ineligible for public office."

President Richard Nixon was forced to resign the presidency because he was caught lying to the American public about being complicit in a cover-up related to the Watergate break-in. He spent the rest of his life writing and lecturing under the cloud of that lie, never able to escape it and return to the full sunlight of truth.

When President Bill Clinton looked into the camera and unambiguously denied an affair with Monica Lewinsky, he was lying. Although that did not cost him his job, it did cost him the public's trust and rendered him significantly less effective in the last two years of his second term. Even today, it is the first thing that comes to mind for many Americans when they hear his name.

While it is still too early to say how Barack Obama's presidency will be remembered, it is undoubtedly true that his lack of honesty in selling ObamaCare contributed to what he himself called a "shellacking" in the 2010 midterm elections. Heritage scholar Robert Moffit observed on the eve of those elections:

> The latest polls show that six out of ten American voters favor outright repeal of ObamaCare. And who can blame them? Who really believes that over the next 10 years Congress will enhance the solvency of Medicare, create two new entitlement programs, secure an estimated $575 billion in "savings" through Medicare payment cuts, preserve access to Medicare benefits, spend an additional $1 trillion to expand coverage, and reduce the deficit? If you do, congratulations! You qualify for membership in the Flat Earth Society. . . .
>
> [President Obama claimed] that if you like your current health plan and benefits, nothing will change. It's transparently untrue. . . . Independent analysts, including the government Actuary at the Department of Health and Human Services, have projected that millions of Americans will lose or be transitioned out of their employer-based coverage.[3]

Nothing can damage a politician's reputation more than being caught in a lie, and that is how it should be. Americans value honesty and recognize dishonesty, and our leaders underestimate their discernment at their peril.

How many politicians have had their careers ruined by lies? The number is impossible to calculate since it's difficult to know what is in the minds of voters when they close the curtain in the voting booth. But it is undoubtedly significant. The political careers of New York governor Eliot Spitzer and South Carolina governor Mark Sanford—two men thought to be top prospects for their party's future nomination for president—met untimely ends through lies about extramarital affairs.

Spitzer, who fancied himself a crusader against corruption, was forced to resign when his frequenting of prostitutes was made public. Sanford, often seen as a leader in moral conservatism, became a pariah when it was revealed that he was having an affair with a woman from Argentina. In both cases it was not the act itself that spelled doom; it was the dishonesty. After all, if someone is willing to betray his spouse in a way he swore before his family, his friends, and God not to do, how can he continue in a position of trust?

Redemption

In the world of politics, nothing is ever final—not victory, not defeat, and not even the loss of the public's trust. Redemption is always a possibility. Contrary to F. Scott Fitzgerald's declaration that "there are no second acts in American lives," the American public is nothing if not forgiving of the shortcomings or mistakes of others. We understand that no one is perfect, and imperfection is perhaps the one trait all human beings share. It's all about how we handle and address those imperfections that determines whether we will have a second act.

Whittaker Chambers was a Communist when he was a young man. In point of fact, he was a member of the American

Communist underground. From 1932 until 1937, Chambers spied for the Soviet Union against his own country. In the ordinary course of events, Chambers would forever be stained with the scarlet letter of treason, but that was not to be his fate.

When Chambers came to his senses, he not only did a mea culpa; he also exposed spies whom he'd worked with during his traitorous days. He did so with immunity, but he still took a huge risk. Would admitting his past publicly cause him to be ostracized and ruin his career? He knew he would avoid prison, but being an outcast in your own country is in itself being in a form of prison. Yet Chambers did not remain silent.

In "A Letter to My Children," Chambers explained who he was:

> I was a witness. I do not mean a witness for the government or against Alger Hiss and the others. Nor do I mean the short, squat, solitary figure, trudging through the impersonal halls of public buildings to testify before Congressional committees, grand juries, loyalty boards, courts of law. A man is not primarily a witness *against* something. That is only incidental to the fact that he is a witness *for* something. A witness, in the sense that I am using the word, is a man whose life and faith are so completely one that when the challenge comes to step out and testify for his faith, he does so, disregarding all risks, accepting all consequences.[4]

Chambers was willing to accept the consequences of his past mistakes. Not everyone believed him when he accused a former high-ranking State Department official, Alger Hiss, of being a

Soviet agent (at least until 1995, when newly declassified Soviet documents confirmed Chambers's charges), but many did.

After resigning from his job as senior editor at *Time* magazine, Chambers wrote his autobiography, *Witness*, which became a huge best seller. He spent the rest of his life a hero to the anti-Communist movement, writing for *National Review*, *Fortune*, and *Life* magazines and inspiring a liberal New Deal Democrat named Ronald Reagan to switch his political allegiance and become a conservative.

The Risk of Honesty

It is impossible to know how people will react to the truth, but true honesty requires that it be told. In 1982, the nation was struck with fear as seven people in the Chicago area were murdered by a cowardly and unknown assailant who struck arbitrarily through poisoning Extra Strength Tylenol capsules with potassium cyanide. As fear coursed through America from coast to coast, Tylenol, the number one nonaspirin pain reliever in the country, saw sales plummet. Johnson & Johnson, the company that manufactures Tylenol, was in a bind. What to do?

Johnson & Johnson CEO James Burke stepped up and took the lead. He apologized for the murders, offered a $100,000 reward for the killer, and recalled all Tylenol capsules across the country. In the article "Tylenol's Maker Shows How to Respond to Crisis," the *Washington Post* reported:

> What J&J executives have done is communicate the message that the company is candid, contrite and compassionate, committed to solving the murders and protecting the public.

The temptation to disclaim any possible connection between the product and the murders must have been difficult for the manufacturer to resist, yet there is no evidence J&J even considered trying to tough it out.

Burke had not tried to avoid responsibility, spin the story, or lie about what was happening. He did what *Time* magazine said "will probably be studied in business schools for a long time to come": he told the truth and spent $50 million to recall all Tylenol capsules from across the country. Within a year the tainted Tylenol brand had regained 80 percent of the market share it had before the murders. Burke's courage, leadership, and honesty were rewarded with the resurgence of what most thought was a doomed brand. Today, Tylenol is considered a trusted name by consumers.

Not everyone who tells the truth runs the risk of bankruptcy, a lawsuit, or loss of a job. Most honest actions are simply people acting in ways that are not in their self-interest and choosing to do the right thing. One such example happened in 1940 on a frozen football field in Hanover, New Hampshire.

Coming into the game, the Big Red Bears of Cornell University were undefeated and ranked second in the nation by the Associated Press. The Indians of Dartmouth were a less-than-stellar team. All signs pointed to another Cornell victory.

Dartmouth had managed to hold off Cornell the entire game, keeping them off the scoreboard while scoring a field goal in the second half. With less than a minute to go in the game, Cornell had the ball on the six-yard line of Dartmouth with a first down. In a hurry-up offense, Cornell finally scored in a frenzy on fourth down.

Upon reviewing the game, officials discovered they had

accidentally given Cornell an extra fifth down at the end of the game, the down on which they scored the winning touchdown. Since the score was recorded and the game was over, it was going to stand. Cornell was going to remain undefeated and in good position to make a run at a national championship. But that would not have been honest.

Upon learning that a mistake was made and that the score would stand, the players, coaches, and athletic director, along with the president of Cornell, decided that the mistake should *not* stand. They sent a telegram to Dartmouth offering to forfeit the game, the only way to change the official outcome. Dartmouth accepted, and the results were reversed.

Cornell had nothing to gain by the forfeit but a lot to lose. Winning by any means other than through fair play was not actually winning to the people at Cornell. It was not honorable; the ends did not justify the means.

This game is now known as the "Five Down Game," and it's used as an example of sportsmanship and honesty to this day. This act of honesty has outlived most of the people there that day. It was a sound decision made generations ago that still reverberates in society today.

The price of being honest cannot truly be known until the bill comes, but it must be paid. Without honesty the very fabric of society is torn just a little. Although every lie does not lead to the downfall of civilization, it adds to the breakdown of trust, which is the oil that coats the gears of society. Without trust, personal and professional relationships stagnate.

"A man is only as good as his word," as the old saying goes, and a nation is only as strong as its people. A strong people, a strong nation, must be willing to be honest with one another and with themselves.

Thomas Paine stated in *The Age of Reason*, "It is impossible to calculate the moral mischief, if I may so express it, that mental lying has produced in society. When a man has so far corrupted and prostituted the chastity of his mind as to subscribe his professional belief to things he does not believe he has prepared himself for the commission of every other crime."[5]

Telling little white lies and tempering the truth to spare someone's feelings are understandable, but the full-blown lie for personal and/or professional gain damages society. The more acceptance lying gains in our lives, the more acceptable lies will become. Redemption through contrition can redeem one's character, but all too often true contrition (as opposed to the repositioning favored by politicians) is lacking. We must, as a nation, embrace the truth teller, no matter how unpleasant the truth may be.

The Abolition of Man

In recent years, however, the very notion that objective truth exists has come under sustained attack. New and influential academic fads—postmodernism, poststructuralism, deconstructionism, relativism, and multiculturalism—urge us to abandon such quaint notions as moral truth, human dignity, and God-given rights, to recognize that reality is "socially constructed," and to view all our ideas through the distorting prisms of race, class, and gender. In such an intellectual climate, people who insist that their beliefs are true become objects of derision, and the dividing lines between right and wrong, good and evil, truth and falsehood grow increasingly blurred and uncertain.[6]

"Several years ago," former education secretary William J. Bennett told a Heritage audience,

> Saul Bellow wrote that "our post-industrial, post-Christian, post-everything period of flux and crisis does not breed stingable horses, only millions of gadflies." Today, we have millions more gadflies and not enough stingable horses. What is a stingable horse? It is a person who stands for the truth in whatever arena he finds himself and who endures however strong the sting—people like Pope John Paul II and Aleksander Solzhenitsyn, Martin Luther King, Margaret Thatcher, and Ronald Wilson Reagan.[7]

Personal truth, professional truth, political truth, spiritual truth—each is as important as the other, and all are important threads in the tapestry of our country. Once you pull out one of those threads, the rest will unravel. Or as the British medievalist and literary critic C. S. Lewis presciently warned in a series of lectures delivered in 1943 and published as *The Abolition of Man*, "We make men without chests and expect of them virtue and enterprise. We laugh at honor and are shocked to find traitors in our midst. We castrate and bid the geldings be fruitful."[8]

Weaving an unwavering commitment to the truth into the fabric of our everyday lives is the surest way to strengthen the American Spirit and guarantee its survival for generations to come.

CHAPTER 9

Something for Nothing

There is no such thing as a free lunch.

—Milton Friedman

Politics is ultimately about competing ideas and visions, so it's not surprising that the greatest divisions in American politics are philosophical in nature. For example, some Americans believe in the founding principle that individuals are responsible for their own well-being and will voluntarily aid those in need. Others believe that people should be *required* to take care of their fellow citizens. This latter group aims to use the power of the state to enforce its belief.

Thus, one group believes in personal responsibility and private charity; the other imposes charity, with the threat of prison behind it, on the productive sector of the economy through taxation and the redistribution of wealth. Not only does this second approach constitute a threat to liberty, but giving someone something for nothing on a regular basis ends up hurting the very person it was meant to help! As Benjamin Franklin put it in *Poor Richard's Almanack*, "God helps them that help themselves."[1]

The fact is, once someone loses the habit of fending for himself, it becomes difficult for him to reacquire it, and he becomes dependent on the state for the rest of his life. And what's true for individuals also holds for corporations: once they start looking to the government for bailouts, they, too, lose their ability to compete in the free market and become wards of Washington. The threats to our liberty, our economy, and our future from this bailout culture can hardly be overstated.

Moral Hazard

Moral hazard occurs when decision makers are insulated from the consequences of their decisions. People behave differently when they are not held responsible for the consequences of their actions. These morally hazardous actions can impose huge costs on the principles themselves, as well as on the rest of us.

Examples of moral hazard abound. Newspapers routinely contain stories of the latest Hollywood star having a run-in with the law or causing a scene at some hot spot by acting outrageously. Yet these people continue to make millions of dollars because they are considered to be bankable stars. How many arrests does it take before a celebrity faces serious consequences? Or consider the false celebrity so many strive to obtain on modern "reality" shows, programs that have one thing in common: they're completely detached from reality.

Remember Tareq and Michaele Salahi? They became over-night sensations by slipping into a White House state dinner without invitations and in violation of security regulations. One might have expected them to fade into (deserved) obscurity after that. Instead, they spent the next year popping up all over the place: on reality television, on daytime talk shows, in tabloid newspapers. What had they accomplished, exactly, to deserve such exposure? They hadn't created any jobs, helped anyone in need, or made a difference in anyone's life. Yet they enjoyed the trappings of fame and presumably of fortune.

When a culture places such a high value on celebrity, celebrities are insulated and shielded from the results of their actions. Having access to the best lawyers, they often escape punishment when they break the law. As long as they are "hot" they are seemingly invulnerable and are surrounded by hangers-on who don't dare tell them no for fear of losing their access. They are potential disasters waiting to happen. Not every star falls victim to the trappings of fame, but many do. There are all too many actors, musicians, and other celebrities who have died tragically or ended up in prison once their stars started to fade, and their lives are striking examples of moral hazard at work.

A larger-scale example of moral hazard occurs in our welfare system. Starting in the 1960s, the federal government declared war on poverty. In the course of this war, as social critic Irving Kristol observed,

> the welfare state came gradually to be seen less as a help-ing hand for those in need, a "safety net," and more as a

communal exercise in compassion toward an ever-expanding proportion of the population. . . . This version of the welfare state was officially recognized, and inaugurated and financed, by Lyndon Johnson. There is considerable evidence in the memoirs of his White House staff that LBJ had no clear idea of what he was doing. That did not, of course, matter.[2]

What did matter was that the War on Poverty, while expensive, created negative incentives. Instead of encouraging the growth of healthy families, the welfare system broke up families. Mothers could receive larger payments from Uncle Sam if they remained single than if they married the father of their child.

Over time, many fatherless children entered the world. The welfare checks showed up month after month, regardless of how their mothers and fathers spent their days. As these boys and girls grew up without fathers around, they came to regard such households as natural. The social safety net designed to be a temporary help to people in need had become a trap dooming them to lives of permanent dependency.

To quote Kristol once again:

It may not be literally true that dependency (like power) tends to corrupt and that absolute dependency (like absolute power) corrupts absolutely. But there is truth enough in that proposition to give pause. After all, how else to explain the fact that the increasing breakdown of the black ghetto family and the proliferation of all sorts of social and individual pathologies parallel so neatly, in time and place, the institution of all those social programs? The people who devised, legislated, and applied those programs surely expected no such consequences and are now at a loss for an explanation. It's reasonable, however, to take seriously the possibility that the two phenomena have a causal connection.[3]

This situation continued for three, even four generations—until 1996, when a Republican Congress passed historic welfare reform legislation (over President Clinton's veto—twice) that began turning things around. The "intellectual godfather" of welfare reform (as *National Review* editor Rich Lowry dubbed him) is Robert Rector, a national authority on poverty and a Heritage Foundation Senior Fellow. Rector played a major role in transforming the Aid to Families with Dependent Children (AFDC) program from a cash welfare program into a jobs program known as Temporary Assistance for Needy Families (TANF). Recipients were required to perform at least twenty to thirty hours per week of work or job preparation activities in exchange for the cash benefit.

The results? Overnight, welfare agencies became job placement offices, and people who had been trapped in dependence began seeking employment. Between 1996 and 2009, caseloads dropped from 4.5 million families to 1.7 million. Employment for single mothers also increased dramatically.

But Rector's work is far from done. Today, the federal government runs more than seventy means-tested antipoverty programs providing cash, food, housing, and social services to low-income persons, but fails to help the recipients become able to provide for themselves. As a result, Rector wrote: "Over the next decade, the U.S. will spend more than $10.3 trillion on means-tested welfare. This amounts to around $100,000 for each person in the lowest-income third of the population. The continuing rapid growth of welfare spending is unsustainable. The U.S. can no longer afford the automatic and unlimited growth of welfare entitlements."[4]

Bailout Culture

But moral hazard doesn't affect only individuals; it has seeped into the very heart of capitalism—the business community. The great conservative journalist and editor William F. Buckley Jr. observed in 1975 that America was tilting to the left, led by American capitalists "fleeing into the protective arms of government at the least hint of commercial difficulty."[5]

That is why conservatives oppose corporate bailouts. Heritage scholars Stuart Butler, Alison Acosta Fraser, and James Gattuso addressed this issue:

> As a general principle, the federal government should not intervene to stave off the consequences of unwise business decisions—even when those decisions are influenced by bad incentives or regulations emanating from the government. Bailing out firms that have miscalculated in the market shoulders taxpayers with costs that should be borne instead by those who made the mistakes. And any indication from government that it will save one group of investors encourages others to line up for help, and the prospect of ultimate protection induces many more to make riskier business decisions—a phenomenon that economists refer to as "moral hazard."[6]

Heritage scholars were especially critical of the Bush administration's decision to siphon $17.4 billion away from the Troubled Assets Relief Program (TARP)—designed to maintain the liquidity of credit markets in the wake of the great financial meltdown of 2008—in order to bail out General Motors and Chrysler. Stuart Butler declared, "The only way to prevent further misuse of the [TARP] program is to abolish it."[7] More generally, prominent scholars and some political leaders have argued that "companies should be allowed to fail, and laws and regulations should create no expectations of a future bailout."[8] If government accedes to the special pleading of corporate lobbyists and ensures corporations against irresponsible behavior, it will only encourage more irresponsible corporate behavior—and more corporate bailouts—in the future.

Enforcement

To put the matter very plainly, there is no such thing as something for nothing. All money, goods, and services must be created through someone's hard and diligent work. The only way a person's hard-earned money and property can be taken away from him is through coercion—force or the threat of fines and imprisonment—put in place by politicians buying voters' loyalty through legislation.

Much of politics today has come to resemble an auction. The politician goes into the political marketplace and offers free money in exchange for votes. His opponent has to increase his bid if he wants to win the election. He therefore offers more free money than his rival. The critical variables are how much free money the politicians will offer, which voters will get the free money, and which unlucky taxpayers will have their hard-earned money taken away from them.

Government has no money. It produces nothing, so it earns nothing. Government has only money it takes from taxpayers or borrows against the payments of future taxpayers. Everything government gives to one person or organization must be taken from another person or organization. Every dollar government "gives" to someone, it must first take from someone else and then deduct carrying costs before passing it on in exchange for votes in the next election.

Charity at the point of a gun, or under threat of prison or punishment, is not real charity. Thomas Jefferson once said, "The natural progress of things is for liberty to yield, and government to gain ground." That is what we see taking place through the government's embrace of moral hazard. The problem is that good politics (doing whatever is necessary to gain reelection) and good policy (holding individuals and institutions responsible for their actions) do not always coincide.

Back to Basics

We need to return to some very old, very basic truths. And one of the most basic truths of all is that there can be no freedom without responsibility. In the words of Nobel laureate F. A. Hayek: "Liberty not only means that the individual has both the opportunity and the burden of choice; it also means that he must bear the consequences of his actions and will receive praise or blame for them."[9]

That people "must bear the consequences of [their] actions" applies to everyone: to humble welfare recipients, who should be required to work or to prepare for work as a condition for receiving aid; and to haughty corporate giants who should be allowed to fail when they flunk the free market test. Welfare programs should create no sense of entitlement to an endless stream of checks; business laws and regulations should create no expectations of future bailouts. Otherwise, the soaring costs of welfare payments, on the one hand, and the endless cycle of corporate failures and bailouts, on the other, will eventually ruin us both morally and financially.

A "something for nothing" approach begets a culture of subservience and dependence and undermines self-reliance, self-discipline, and self-respect—traditional virtues that have always been vital components of the American Spirit.

CHAPTER 10

Faith

Freedom sees in religion the companion of its struggles and its triumphs, the cradle of its infancy, the divine source of its rights. It considers religion as the safeguard of mores; and mores as the guarantee of laws and the pledge of its duration.

—Alexis de Tocqueville

We hold these Truths to be self-evident, that all Men are created equal, that they are endowed by their Creator with certain unalienable Rights, that among these are Life, Liberty, and the Pursuit of Happiness.

—Declaration of Independence

Respecting Faith

Faith has always played a major role in American history. From our Founding Fathers to politicians today, acknowledgment of

God in public speeches is commonplace in American discourse. In a letter he wrote to his wife, Abigail, the day the Declaration of Independence was approved by the Continental Congress, John Adams wrote that July Fourth "ought to be commemorated as the day of deliverance by solemn acts of devotion to God Almighty." But while the United States was founded by men with a deep and abiding belief in a Christian God, they took great care to ensure that any and all religions would be respected and protected by the Constitution.

Today, however, the Founders' attitude to religion is widely misunderstood. A major source of confusion is the phrase "separation of church and state," used by President Thomas Jefferson in an 1802 letter to the Danbury Baptist Association of Connecticut. Many have interpreted this phrase to mean that religion should be entirely personal, kept out of schools and other public institutions. But as Heritage scholar Jennifer Marshall has argued, this interpretation is incorrect:

> Jefferson wanted to protect states' freedom of religion from federal government control and religious groups' freedom to tend to their internal matters of faith and practice without government interference generally. Unfortunately, Jefferson's phrase is probably more widely known than the actual text of the Constitution's First Amendment: "Congress shall make no law respecting the establishment of religion, or prohibiting the free exercise thereof."[1]

America's Founding Fathers did not want the government to impose a government-sponsored church on all Americans, but neither did they seek to confine religion to a separate, private sphere of life. On the contrary, they believed that religion had a vital and enduring role to play in the public affairs of the new American republic. To cite Marshall again:

> The Founders argued that virtue derived from religion is indispensable to limited government. . . . The American model of religious liberty takes a strongly positive view of religious practice, both private and public. . . . Far from privatizing religion, it assumes that religious believers and institutions will take active roles in society, including engaging in politics and policy-making and helping form the public's moral consensus. In fact, the American Founders considered religious engagement in shaping the public morality essential to ordered liberty and the success of their experiment in self-government.[2]

Faith and Liberty

We Americans are rightly proud of our tradition of political and economic liberty. But is an individual's freedom to choose a sufficient guarantee of a good society? Our Founders did not think so, and neither do we. Social critic Irving Kristol observed:

> According to conservative thought, a market economy cannot work except in a society comprised of people who are, in sufficient degree, bourgeois—that is, people who are orderly, law-abiding, and diligent, and who resolutely defer gratification, sexual as well as financial, so that, despite the freedom

granted each individual, the future nonetheless continues to be nourished at the expense of the present. For people of this kind to lead lives of this kind, it seems to be the case that religion is indispensable. This appears to be a sociological truth. It is religion that reassures people that this world of ours is a home, not just a habitat, and that the tragedies and unfairness we all experience are features of a more benign, if not necessarily comprehensible, whole. It is religion that restrains the self-seeking hedonistic impulse so easily engendered by a successful market economy.[3]

One of the clearest expressions of the Founders' attitude to religion—endorsed by most Americans today—came from our second president, John Adams. "Our Constitution was made only for a moral and religious people," Adams declared in 1798. "It is wholly inadequate to the government of any other."[4] Only a moral and religious people could acquire and retain such traits of character as honesty, kindness, thoughtfulness, respect for law, fairness, self-discipline, and self-reliance—virtues the Founders rightly deemed necessary for self-rule.

Resisting Oppression

The Founders had learned from history that religious despotism enforced by government was a recipe for oppression. "Spiritual freedom is the root of political liberty," Thomas Paine stated. They were starting a new type of country that had never existed before, one where individual liberty was recognized and respected by the state. People being free to worship in a manner of their choosing, or not to worship at all, was perhaps the most important aspect of that liberty. Moreover, people could change their religious views and proselytize their neighbors without government interference.

Throughout history monarchs and governments have forced particular religions on their people. Hoping to conceive a male heir, King Henry VIII of England wanted the Catholic Church to annul his marriage to Catherine of Aragon and allow him to marry Anne Boleyn. When the pope denied his request, Henry set about applying pressure to make it happen anyway. Eventually Henry broke with the Catholic Church and created the Church of England, declaring himself its "Supreme Head." Henry's decision had essentially imposed a new religion on a people who were, to that point, mostly Catholic. Chaos ensued.

Henry's Lord Chancellor, Thomas More, was executed for refusing to swear an oath that was critical of the pope and recognized Henry's supremacy. England's state religion thereafter was decided by the monarch, as head of the church. The monarch's preference between Catholicism and Protestantism was a life-or-death issue. By the time of the American Revolution, it had changed several times. The Founding Fathers were aware of this history and the turmoil it caused. And they were aware of other examples of religious intolerance. Moreover, they were members of several denominations and creeds. They wanted to avoid actions that had led to untold suffering. As a practical matter, they knew that the new federal government could never agree to support any particular sect.

In the American model of religious liberty that the Founders designed, a person's relationship with God was between him and his Maker. It was not a matter for government intervention. Believers could influence government through participation in the political process, but government could not dictate the content of religious belief. By keeping government out of religion, the Founders fostered an atmosphere of tolerance and acceptance that makes the United States a pillar of diversity of faiths in the community of nations and, at the same time, one of the most religious nations on the planet.

A Pilot's Faith

No matter what their religious beliefs, no one can deny that faith in a higher power is a powerful force in life. Stories abound of people enduring unimaginable hardships with little more than their belief in God to sustain them. Here is one of them:

Before John McCain was a candidate for president or senator from Arizona, he was a warrior. In Vietnam, Lieutenant McCain, a fighter pilot, was shot down and taken prisoner. For seven years he was tortured in a prison camp known as the Hanoi Hilton. Pushed to the edge many times, McCain relied on his faith to keep him strong.

In his autobiography, *Faith of My Fathers*, McCain recounted some of the horrors he had to endure and depicted his torture at the hands of merciless North Vietnamese prison guards. But there was one guard who helped McCain survive through simple acts of kindness.

After a horrible session of torture, where McCain was tied up in a manner designed to choke him and was left that way all night, this guard, whom McCain called his "Good Samaritan," sneaked into his cell and loosened the ropes. He returned in the morning to retighten them so as to avoid getting caught. Later, on Christmas Day, the guard approached McCain and drew a cross in the dirt in front of him in the prison's courtyard. After a few moments, the man rubbed it out and went on his way.

This show of faith and display of kindness were made possible by the faith the two men shared. Referring to the gospel, McCain wrote, "That message can reach into any place, however dark. Even in solitary confinement, when everything else has been taken away, nothing can separate us from the love of our Creator."

Four Chaplains' Day

Most Americans have never heard of Four Chaplains' Day and have no idea why Congress should have designated February 3 by this title. But on February 3, 1943, the Allied ship *Dorchester* was hit by a torpedo fired by a Nazi submarine off the icy waters of Greenland. As the crew of the Dorchester prepared to abandon ship, four chaplains—a priest, a rabbi, and two Protestant ministers—distributed life jackets. When no life jackets were left, the chaplains removed their jackets and gave them to four young sailors. As the *Dorchester* went down, the chaplains embraced and bowed their heads in prayer. It is their courage that we recall every February 3.

On February 7, 1954, President Dwight Eisenhower saluted the chaplains' courage and the faith that was the source of their courage:

We remember that . . . aboard the transport *Dorchester*, four chaplains of four faiths together willingly sacrificed their lives so that four others might live.

In the three centuries that separate the Pilgrims of the Mayflower from the chaplains of the *Dorchester*, America's freedom, her courage, her strength, and her progress have had their foundation in faith.

President Eisenhower concluded: "Today as then, there is need for positive acts of renewed recognition that faith is our surest strength, our greatest resource."[5]

A Religious Nation

Religious liberty is as characteristic of America as our democratic political system and our free market economy. Nowhere in the world is there more religious diversity, with all manner of faiths existing in relative harmony in the same neighborhoods, and with different houses of worship sharing the same streets in many cases. History is filled with wars based on religious difference, yet in the United States these problems, with rare exceptions, are a distant memory.

In the United States no religions are given preferential treatment over others. Crimes motivated by religious hatred are significantly lower here than, say, in Nigeria, where as many as twelve thousand Nigerians have been killed in a dozen Christian-Muslim clashes since 1999.[6]

Immediately following the September 11 attacks, attacks that were facilitated, planned, and executed by followers of a radicalized and politicized version of Islam, the United States could have easily repeated the mistakes of the past. After Pearl Harbor, President Franklin Delano Roosevelt created internment camps for Japanese Americans, essentially imprisoning them without trial for the duration of the war. Undoubtedly the urge was there in some, wrapped in fear, to do something similar with Muslim Americans. But we did not. Indeed, we did not take steps to infringe on the rights of Muslims in the United States, and we took great care to ensure they were not treated any differently than they had been before. This stands in vivid contrast with some nations in the Middle East, where Christians, Jews, Hindus, and other non-Muslims are forbidden to share their faith or even meet publicly for worship.

On September 20, 2001, just nine days after the attacks, President George W. Bush addressed a joint session of Congress to discuss the state of the nation and what we, as a nation, were going to do in response to those attacks. We knew at that point that the terrorist organization al-Qaeda, with its radicalized view of Islam, had orchestrated the attacks. At a moment of anger and pain, President Bush took care to convey a message of friendship to the Muslim world. "The enemy of America is not our many Muslim friends. It is not our many Arab friends. Our enemy is a radical network of terrorists and every government that supports them," he said that night.

In reassuring Muslims of America's continuing friendship, President Bush shed light on one of the great pillars of our national character. We do not judge a person by his faith; we judge individuals by their actions. President Bush spent a great deal of the rest of his tenure reaching out to the Muslim world and offering the hand of friendship to anyone who would accept it.

Freedom "of" Religion Is Not Freedom "from" Religion

Along with the freedom to worship in the manner of our choosing is the right to refrain from worship. In the absence of a national religion, people are free to choose, or not choose, any religion that touches them. The choice not to practice any religion or believe in a God is, in the eyes of the law, as valid a choice as any other. But some people have taken that freedom and twisted the meaning of the First Amendment in an attempt to purge any recognition of God from public life. George Washington warned against this in his Farewell Address to the nation, saying, "Whatever may be conceded to the influence of refined education on minds of peculiar structure, reason and experience both forbid us to expect, that national morality can prevail in exclusion of religious principle."[7]

Atheism is the belief that there is no God. People are free to choose to believe this and live their lives accordingly. Unfortunately some people who exercise their right not to practice any religion, as well as some who publicly proclaim their faith, have sought to purge any expression of faith from the public square.

The Reverend Billy Graham said, "The framers of our Constitution meant we were to have freedom of religion, not freedom from religion," meaning that nonbelievers have no more right to impose their convictions on people of faith than people of faith have to impose the reverse. But that has not stopped some from attempting to use the power of the courts to impose a secular, atheistic belief system on government.

Groups such as the People for the American Way, Americans United for Separation of Church and State, and countless left-wing organizations work tirelessly and spend millions of dollars supporting lawsuits seeking to remove any reference to God, the Ten Commandments, or even crosses on any public grounds. There was even a push to ban the Pledge of Allegiance because of the phrase "under God."

These activists are not interested in tolerance; they are interested in advancing their agenda. Just as imposing God through government is wrong, purging God from government is equally wrong.

Antireligious activists often cite the "separation of church and state" as justification for banning things such as "In God We Trust" from our currency. You hear that phrase all the time, no doubt, to justify the removal of a nativity scene or a menorah from a town hall front lawn around Christmas or Hanukkah. It's referred to as if it's gospel itself or at least in the Constitution. The only problem is that it's not in the Constitution, explicitly or implicitly. On the contrary, as Heritage's Matthew Spalding has pointed out,

> While the Constitution officially "separates" church and state at the level of doctrine and lawmaking, it also allows the general (nonsectarian) encouragement and support of religion in public laws, in official speeches and ceremonies, on public property and in public buildings, and even in public

schools. Such activities were understood to be part of "the free exercise of religion."[8]

We separate religion and government to stop government from picking a religion and forcing it on everyone else; we do not outlaw the acknowledgment of God in government. Each session of Congress is opened with a prayer, as is the Supreme Court. Hardly a speech by any president ends without the words "May God bless the United States." President Bill Clinton, nearly echoing the words of Rev. Graham, said, "Sometimes I think the environment in which we operate is entirely too secular. The fact that we have freedom of religion doesn't mean we need to try to have freedom from religion." Or to cite Ronald Reagan, "Freedom prospers when religion is vibrant and the rule of law under God is acknowledged."

The acknowledgment of faith is not the imposition of it. The United States has a long history of tolerance and acceptance of all religious beliefs, even atheism. The move to purge any acknowledgment of a higher power will always have supporters, and they have the right to advocate their views, but to claim that those views are supported by the Constitution is to seriously misinterpret both our history and what the document itself says.

Faith has played an invaluable role in our nation's history, from the founding of our nation to the present day. The freedom to believe in God or not, and to choose which religion to follow, is fundamental to our personal liberty. Attempts have and always will be made to remove faith from the public square, but they must be met with even stronger resolve to retain it.

Heritage scholar Ryan Messmore emphasized that "religious communities bind people vertically to God and horizontally to one another. These social bonds not only depend on, they also help to generate, trust, cooperation, respect for authority, self-sacrifice, and a shared pursuit of, and participation in, the common good."[9]

Faith has always been an integral part of American society. Indeed, Alexis de Tocqueville went so far as to call religion "the first of America's political institutions," because although it "never mixes directly in the government of society," it nevertheless determines the "habits of the heart" of all Americans.[10] Whether you choose to worship or not, or however you choose to worship, everyone benefits from the interweaving of faith into our societal fabric. To eliminate it from the public discourse would deny our history and remove a crucial component of the American Spirit.

CHAPTER 11

The Law

You're (probably) a federal criminal.

—Alex Kozinski, chief judge of the Court
of Appeals for the Ninth Circuit

My guiding principle is this: Guilt is never to be doubted.

—Franz Kafka

The Law

Our system of laws creates a structure, a framework of peace, order, and security in which people are free to be and do what they like. The greatness of America can be found in our legal system, which is aimed at safeguarding the rights of all citizens. Americans accused of crimes have a presumption of innocence and a constitutional right not to testify in their own defense. The burden of proof lies squarely with the prosecutor, with the state, to prove someone guilty "beyond a reasonable doubt."

Like our overall structure of government, our justice system is designed to protect our rights against encroachment by the state.

Equality Under the Law

At one time in history, there was a general belief in the divine right of kings. Whatever the king or ruler decided at that moment was the law. Thus, standards were constantly changing. Because "power tends to corrupt and absolute power corrupts absolutely," in the immortal words of Lord Acton, laws handed down by kings were often arbitrary, unfair, unjust, and cruel.

In America, the Founders recognized that the first requirement for a civil society is order. We enjoy a system of ordered liberty, where the rules are spelled out, written down, and equally applied to everyone. The principle of equality in the Declaration of Independence and the Constitution refers to equality before the law. This is why it is said that in America, justice is blind. Because the law is objective and written down, all Americans are subject to it equally, regardless of their economic or social background.

Are there exceptions or deviations from good decisions based on law? Of course there are, but in our system, the main focus is on fairness, equity, and justice.

Embodied at the core of our justice system is the Founders' adherence to the eighteenth-century British jurist William Blackstone's formulation, paraphrased by Benjamin Franklin as, "It is better one hundred guilty persons should escape than that one innocent person should suffer." The Founders took care to ensure as best as possible that liberty not be denied anyone without the highest level of proof. The system is not perfect— sometimes the guilty go free and the innocent are convicted—but there are the most rigorous safeguards in place to prevent this unfortunate outcome as much as humanly possible.

Or at least, there used to be.

Overcriminalization

Unfortunately, as the size and scope of government have grown, it has become next to impossible for ordinary, law-abiding citizens to carry on their lives and businesses without violating some obscure law and quite possibly going to jail for their "crime." Today, neither the Justice Department nor the Congressional Research Service can even count the number of crimes in federal law, and there is simply no way the average citizen can know what to do in order to avoid becoming a federal criminal. Edwin Meese, who as mentioned earlier now holds the Ronald Reagan Chair in Public Policy at the Heritage Foundation and directs its Center for Legal and Judicial Studies, called attention to this point:

> The modern frenzy of promiscuous lawmaking has turned the criminal law into a giant amorphous mass, impossible to quantify and simply unknowable. Like the mythical Sword of Damocles, it hangs over the heads of morally innocent people, who are unaware of the potential loss of freedom, livelihood, reputation, and family that awaits them when the sword falls. It threatens every aspect of American life, including our economic strength and global competitiveness.[1]

A twentieth-century literary classic is a novel called *The Trial*, written in German by the Czech author Franz Kafka and published in 1925. It tells the story of a man prosecuted by an inaccessible authority for a crime whose nature is never revealed to him. Today, the adjective *Kafkaesque* is often used to describe absurd, nightmarish situations in which an isolated, helpless individual is harassed by remote and inscrutable powers for reasons he can barely fathom.

Although Kafka's *The Trial* was a work of fiction, the Kafkaesque ordeal undergone by honest, law-abiding Abner Schoenwetter, who had the great misfortune of falling afoul of the American judicial system's tendency to overcriminalize unintentional violations of the law, was all too real. Schoenwetter spent sixty-nine months in federal prison for doing something—importing undersized lobsters from Honduras and packaging them in plastic, rather than in boxes, as required by Honduran law—that he never suspected was illegal. On September 28, 2010, he recounted his ordeal before the House Committee on the Judiciary, and while his testimony is lengthy, we are reproducing it virtually in full because the story he tells is not only shocking but (we would hope) profoundly un-American.

Testimony of Abner Schoenwetter

Looking at my story objectively, it is relatively hard to explain how this all happened to me. I am and have always been a quiet, hardworking, law-abiding, family man . . .

I have been in the commercial seafood business since 1986. I met one of my codefendants, David Henson McNab, that year and we struck up an arrangement where I would buy his catches of lobster tails and resell them. . . . Little did I know, however, that a single boatload of Honduran lobsters would soon turn my dream into a nightmare.

. . . Every one of our shipments always cleared customs and passed FDA inspection even after being held up at times for random sampling and testing.

What was different this time was that David never delivered on the contract because the contents of his ship were seized by the National Marine Fishery Service (NMFS) in Bayou La Batre. . . .

During the next six months, we heard of negotiations between David's attorneys and the attorneys for the government. In fact, my lawyer was told that a deal had been struck between David and the federal government, whereby the government would confiscate the percentage of lobster that was said to be in violation of Honduran law and release the balance . . Not long after this incident, a similar group of federal agents came to my house at 6:00 in the morning to arrest me. They found only my son and his girlfriend there as I was in North Carolina at the time. After threatening my son with arrest if he did not tell them where I was, he called me and I had my attorney contact them at the house and agree that I would self-surrender in Mobile, Alabama. The government was treating my family like I was a suspected murderer rather than a seafood purchaser. I couldn't believe it. After my arrest, I eventually found out that I was being charged with smuggling and conspiracy based upon violations of Honduran fishing regulations that applied to me under a federal law known as the Lacey Act. I was being prosecuted by the United States government because the lobsters that I had contracted to buy were allegedly in violation of three Honduran administrative rules . . . I was facing multiple years in prison and thousands of dollars in fines if found guilty . . .

Most of my trial dealt with the complex relationship between the Honduran regulations and American law. The issue was so complicated in fact that the judge was forced to hold a separate hearing to determine the validity and meaning of the Honduran rules. Our lawyers presented a great deal of evidence showing that the regulations were invalid and should therefore not be used against us. They presented a letter from the Attorney General of Honduras confirming that the size regulation had never been signed into law by the Honduran president. They also gathered testimony from a former Honduran Minister of Justice discussing how the egg-bearing regulation was primarily directed at turtles and was never meant to apply to lobsters. None of this evidence mattered to the court, however. . . .

. . . Up until this point, I had been convinced that the justice system would sort out the whole mess. Throughout the trial, I had held out hope that the prosecutors and judge would come to their senses, recognize my innocence, and let me get back to my law-abiding life. All of that hope went out the window, however, when the jury found me guilty in November 2000 and the judge later sentenced me to 97 months in prison! In addition, I would have to serve 3 years under supervised release and pay a $15,000 fine and a $100,000 forfeiture, which I had to re-mortgage my house in order to pay . . .

Shortly after the appeal was turned down by the court, I again self-surrendered to the government to begin serving my sentence. I don't want to dwell too long on my time in prison because it is, as you would imagine, a mind-numbing, soul-crushing, life-draining experience. . . .

Taking these facts into consideration, it is still difficult to say whether prison is tougher on the inmate or the inmate's family. In my case, prison certainly ground me down. It made me a far less trusting person and triggered a range of personal health problems that I am dealing with to this day. It also cost me my reputation, my livelihood, and my ability to vote. The toll on my family, however, was perhaps even more immense . . .

On August 27, 2010, I completed the last five months of my six years and three months of confinement at home. I am now under three years of federally supervised release, and the most pressing challenges for me and my family still remain. I struggle daily with how to readjust to life after prison and often find myself reflecting on a number of important per-sonal questions. How do I reconnect with family and friends? Will they view me in the same light as before my time in prison? How do I start my financial life over at age 64 with only Social Security income to depend on?[2]

A Squandered Treasure?

Tragically Abner Schoenwetter's experience is far from unique. There are the father-and-son arrowhead collectors who are now federal criminals because they unknowingly violated the Archaeological Resources Protection Act of 1979; the aspiring inventor who spent fifteen months in prison for environmental crimes, even though he neither harmed nor intended to harm anyone; and the Pennsylvania woman who injured her husband's lover and now faces federal charges related to an international arms-control treaty. Heritage Foundation scholars have compiled many such stories and published them in a book, *One Nation Under Arrest: How Crazy Laws, Rogue Prosecutors, and Activist Judges Threaten Your Liberty.*

Working with the National Association of Criminal Defense lawyers, Heritage scholars have also examined new laws for non-violent crimes enacted by the 109th Congress in 2005 and 2006. Their findings were shocking: of the thirty-six new crimes created by that Congress, 25 percent did not require prosecutors to prove criminal intent, and 40 percent had only a weak criminal intent requirement.[3]

Many national organizations are fighting *overcriminalization*—a recent coinage to describe an alarming trend: treating law-abiding Americans who unintentionally violate some obscure statute, of whose existence they were not even aware, as though they were criminals. An unusual range of organizations, including the American Bar Association, American Civil Liberties Union, Families Against Mandatory Minimums, Manhattan Institute, National Association of Criminal Defense Lawyers, and National Federation of Independent Business, as well as the Heritage Foundation, agrees that a bedrock principle of American criminal law, *mens rea* (Latin for "guilty mind"), which requires the prosecution to prove criminal intent, is being violated by our federal legal system.

This trend must be reversed; distinctions must be made

between innocent mistakes and deliberate crimes; and ambitious prosecutors must be prevented from using the tens or even hundreds of thousands of criminal offenses (no one knows the exact number) contained in federal and state statutes to ruin the lives of ordinary Americans. Otherwise, what happened to Abner Schoenwetter might well happen to any of us some day.

As former attorney general Edwin Meese wrote in his introduction to *One Nation Under Arrest*:

> Many legal scholars—and a large and increasing number of judges and lawyers—now recognize that American criminal law has deteriorated so badly and become so politicized that substantial reform is needed. . . . Taking the necessary steps to ensure that American criminal law once again routinely exemplifies the right principles and purposes will require much work, but the alternative is to squander the great treasure that is the American criminal justice system.[4]

The one-time head of the dreaded Soviet secret police, Lavrentiy Beria, once boasted, "Show me the man, and I'll find you the crime."[5] The American Spirit will never survive such a Kafkaesque transformation of our once-great criminal justice system.

CHAPTER 12

Tolerance and Open-Mindedness

Tolerance always has limits—it cannot tolerate what is itself actively intolerant.

—Sidney Hook

Open Minds

In America, most people start at the bottom and move up in life as a result of hard work and dedication. This common bond is the reason why Americans are some of the most open-minded, tolerant, and accepting people in the world and why people from 194 countries have come to America, "yearning to breathe free."

Ronald Reagan once said, "I consider all proposals for government action with an open mind before voting no." He was, of course, poking fun at himself. Ronald Reagan had one of the most open minds when it came to dealing with individuals, which was one of his biggest keys to success. And open-mindedness is an important key to anyone's success in modern America.

Diversity

Nowhere on earth do more people of different races, creeds, religions, belief systems, and every other characteristic of humanity come together than in the United States. America has never been a homogeneous nation, and that helps explain our strength.

Americans accept one another's differences. We are a melting pot, a nation of people from diverse backgrounds who embrace their commonalities. Those commonalities make up the unique American culture we all share. Beyond that, all of us are free to preserve whatever elements we choose from our diverse heritages.

The trend to maintain a personal culture based on one's heritage generally exists most strongly in new immigrants to this country. The more generations that are born here after an immigrant family arrives, the more they embrace the broader American culture while maintaining, more or less zealously, aspects of their family's heritage. This is the secret sauce of the American culture.

Tolerance

Often today you hear the word *tolerance* used as if it meant acceptance. It does not. To tolerate someone's disagreeable behavior (to you) is an American virtue. To accept someone's disagreeable behavior is to betray yourself. An individual's liberty would never require so great a sacrifice. But the act of tolerance is a crucial component of the freedom every American enjoys.

A person's individual rights stop when he interferes with the rights of others. He is free to disagree with anyone, but he cannot infringe upon another person's rights to do and think as he or she chooses. You can try to convince, you can try to persuade, but you cannot coerce. Agreeing to disagree is as American as apple pie.

The best formulation of tolerance can be found in a quotation from English writer Evelyn Beatrice Hall, who said, "I disapprove of what you say, but I will defend to the death your right to say it."

America was founded on the basis of tolerating differences of religion and national origin. Over time, we have evolved to the point where that virtue has come to include just about every possible human configuration and lifestyle imaginable. Yes, there is still intolerance, but it is in the hearts of individuals, not institutionalized in the law.

Limits to Tolerance?

An especially vexing challenge facing free societies is whether to tolerate totalitarian movements that seek to replace democracy with despotism. When such movements are relatively small and weak, tolerating them appears to be a risk-free option. But if this tolerance enables them to grow and eventually gain power, tolerance can lead to tyranny. "Thus it is," observed philosopher Leszek Kolakowski, "that unlimited tolerance turns against itself and destroys the very conditions of its own existence."[1] Kolakowski believed that political movements seeking to destroy freedom itself should not be tolerated. We agree.

Another dilemma faced by free societies concerns the legitimacy of censorship. Must a tolerant society abandon all resistance to vulgarity and obscenity, or does it have the right to censor the most violent and sexually explicit material now easily available on the Internet, in motion pictures, and even (increasingly) on "family" TV?

According to the eminent jurist Judge Robert Bork, the notion that censorship is un-American is quite recent:

> From the earliest colonies on this continent over 300 years ago, and for about 175 years of our existence as a nation, we endorsed and lived with censorship. We do not have to imagine what censorship might be like; we know from experience. Some of it was formal, written in statutes or city ordinances; some of it was informal, as in the movie producers' agreement to abide by the rulings of the Hayes office. Some of it was inevitably silly—the rule that the movies could not show even a husband and wife fully dressed on a bed unless each had one foot on the floor—and some of it was no doubt pernicious. The period of Hayes office censorship was also, perhaps not coincidentally, the golden age of the movies.[2]

Prior to World War II, censorship was a common feature of American life, and the courts generally endorsed it. Social critic Irving Kristol recalled:

> [W]hen I was young, there were burlesque shows, "topless" shows, we would call them, in New York, and Fiorello La Guardia, a very liberal and progressive mayor, decided that

this was not good for the city. He did not want New York City to be known as a center for striptease shows, so he prohibited them. Just like that. The issue was taken to court, and the court ruled that La Guardia was the elected representative of the public, and if the public wanted things that way, it was their right. People who didn't like it could leave New York City and move to Newark, where you could go to a burlesque show. There was no outraged public debate, no crisis, no book written on the subject. In the United States in that era, any community that wanted to order its public life in a certain way was permitted to do so. One's position had to be "within reason," but the point is that the range of issues which one could reasonably decide one way or another was considered to be quite broad, and open to a process of political trial and error.[3]

Today, of course, no New York mayor would even consider banning a topless show, and if he tried, the courts would never allow him to succeed.

As Judge Bork observed, "Under today's constitutional doctrine, it would be difficult to impossible to punish the lewd and obscene, or the profane. First Amendment jurisprudence has shifted from the protection of the exposition of ideas towards the protection of self-expression—however lewd, obscene, or profane."[4] Judge Bork attributes this shift to the changing values of American judges rather than to a faithful interpretation of the Constitution: "Arguments that society may properly set limits to what may be shown, said, and sung run directly counter to the mood of our cultural elites in general, and in particular the attitude (it is hardly more than that) of our judges, many of whom, most unfortunately, are members in good standing of that elite."[5]

Judge Bork's analysis of the censorship issue points to a larger problem facing our nation—what Heritage scholar Matthew Spalding calls "the new jurisprudence":

> We can see this new jurisprudence expressed in the old and new views of judicial review. The Founders' view was that the Supreme Court in deciding particular cases would consider whether the laws in question were consistent with the text of the Constitution. The new view is that judges should decide according to whether the law comports with their own (not the Constitution's) standards of reasonableness and rationality, shaped by the spirit and course of developing court decisions and constitutional interpretation.[6]

In the historically unprecedented view of many of our most progressive judges, it is reasonable and rational for "artists" to express themselves by incitement to rape and murder; it is unreasonable and irrational for the community to defend itself through censorship. We disagree.

Thought

The ability to think for oneself is undoubtedly the most important of all human attributes. To be open to new ideas, to conceive them and execute them, is the high-octane fuel that drives our economy. Innovation does not occur without an open mind and original thoughts.

What sets someone apart from others? What causes some to succeed beyond others? An indispensable key to success is original thought. Couple that with dreams, original ideas, the courage to try to implement them, hard work, and determination (not to mention some luck), and you pretty much have the recipe for every great American success story. But the first ingredient, the seed from which a mighty oak grows, comes from the freedom to think for oneself. Without it nothing else matters.

The United States is the home of innovation. Nearly every type of product that has improved quality of life the world over—from medicine to computers to entertainment—has its roots in the United States. The freedom we enjoy to dream, to act, and to think has brought about cures for diseases, aid to the disabled and the elderly, and the widespread distribution of necessities that once were luxuries. Henry Ford created the assembly line that made the automobile affordable to all Americans. Dr. Jonas Salk created a vaccine for polio, the plague of the early twentieth century. Bill Gates created the operating system for computers that made them usable and accessible to all the peoples of the world. Americans were the first to reach the moon, invent air-conditioning, transplant organs, and develop many other technologies and advancements.

In nations where liberty is curtailed or controlled by government, innovation is stymied. What innovations or inventions that we use today came from the old Soviet Union? What came from Cuba? Or North Korea?

It is not out of line to say that the United States has directed the course of human history more significantly and positively than any other nation in the history of the world. The key to our success is, always has been, and always will be our liberty. The liberty we enjoy unshackles the mind and nourishes creativity.

The ability to think and to question the status quo should also characterize our attitude to government, but sadly many Americans have come to regard the growing reach of Big Government as a necessity of modern life. As one coauthor of this book said in an address to the Mont Pelerin Society, which, since its founding in 1947, has played a major role in preserving and strengthening economic and political freedom:

> The Founders had a burning faith in the ability of ordinary people to accomplish extraordinary things once they were freed from the fetters of Big Government. But modern Americans, who grew up in a welfare state and became accustomed to delegating so many of life's tasks to a gigantic bureaucracy, simply aren't sure that they can take up the slack on their own. In the absence of Big Government, they ask, who would help the poor? Who would protect the environment? Who would see to the educational needs of our children? Who would guarantee an adequate level of health care? Who would provide a decent living for the old, the sick, and the disadvantaged? Who, in short, would serve as his brother's keeper—if not Big Brother himself?[7]

The answer, of course, is that *we* would. We, the people—not we, the helpless, ignorant masses, who cling desperately to our "guns or religion" and anxiously await the arrival of a messiah-president to deliver us from our frustrated, bewildered, and embittered selves.[8]

We Americans need to regain a sense of our own power, ingenuity, and creativity. We need to realize that many of the tasks the public sector performs so poorly today could be performed far better by the private sector tomorrow. We need to understand that there are more compassionate ways of helping the poor; more enlightened ways of protecting the environment; and more effective ways of educating our children, healing our sick, and tending to our elderly than relying on the "invisible foot," as Milton Friedman called it, of a distant, muscle-bound bureaucracy.

In short, we Americans need to open our minds to the untapped potential of freedom, to the hidden strengths of civil society, and to the limitless power of the American Spirit.

CHAPTER 13

Idealistic Realism

The test of an ideal or rather of an idealist, is the power to
hold to it and get one's inspiration from it under difficulties.
When one is comfortable and well off, it is easy to talk high.

—Oliver Wendell Holmes Jr.

Realism

The actress Bette Davis once said, "Hollywood always wanted
me to be pretty, but I fought for realism." Many Americans live
in a fantasy world. They believe things that are obviously not
true and that they usually know, on some level, to be false. To
resolve this cognitive dissonance, they convince themselves that
assertion is proof.

The Founding Fathers were thoroughly knowledgeable
about human nature and took it into account in their discussions and deliberations. The Declaration of Independence is the

embodiment of our ideals. It insisted that "all Men are created equal" decades before the Civil War that would make the concept possible and almost two centuries before the civil rights movement that would make it a reality.

The Constitution is one of the ultimate expressions of American realism. When its architects emerged with it at the end of the Constitutional Convention, the document was referred to as the "Miracle in Philadelphia." America's Founders knew that people generally act in their own interests. They seek personal advantage and are self-oriented and ambitious. It is the way of the world and can be seen in everything from poker to politics. The Constitution sought to control those impulses through a series of checks and balances, so no person or faction could seize complete power.

Assessing the circumstances in which you find yourself and honestly evaluating the options available to you are good business, no matter what your business. They are also smart.

Being a realist means, quite simply, that you acknowledge reality. Novelist Philip K. Dick once described reality as "that which, when you stop believing in it, doesn't go away." Reality does not go away, as much as we might sometimes like it to. Those who can face reality have a better chance of shaping it into something they would like it to resemble.

Being Honest with Yourself

We've already covered the importance of being honest with others, but honesty with oneself is equally important, if not more so. If people cannot admit the truth to themselves, they are certainly incapable of conveying it to others.

"The truth is incontrovertible; malice may attack it, ignorance may deride it, but in the end, there it is." That is the wisdom of Winston Churchill, and like so many of his observations, it stands the test of time. If you cannot admit the truth to yourself, your actions based on your inner lies will bring you no credit. And if you deliberately set out to deceive others, you will by no means escape suffering. In the words of philosopher Leszek Kolakowski, "[W]hile lying is often harmful to other people, it is more often harmful to ourselves, for its effects are soul-destroying."[1]

Every human being should strive to become what Benjamin Ferguson called Abraham Lincoln: "the noblest work of God— an honest man." All of us will fall short of being completely honest, but each person who aspires to that goal and lives a life wrapped around that inspiration will sleep well and build a life of integrity.

Accepting Reality

To improve the status quo—and thus to improve your life—you must first acknowledge the status quo. One of the most difficult things a person can do, especially in rough times, is to take an honest and objective look at himself. On a larger scale, the founding of our country illustrates this process.

The Founding Fathers agreed that England's rule over the colonies was unjust, but they disagreed on how that injustice should be addressed. Some representatives wanted a complete break; others thought reconciliation was still possible. Eventually, through debate, discussion, and soul-searching, each delegate to the Second Continental Congress reached the same conclusion—independence.

For them to move forward and succeed, they needed a firm grasp of reality and a firm grounding in it. The Founders assessed the risks to their families, their fellow countrymen, and themselves and made their decision. In business, risks must be assessed on behalf of employees, shareholders, and self before decisions are made. Realists are painfully honest in their assessments, especially in their self-assessments. You can't know how to get where you're going until you're certain you know where you are.

Not everyone is capable of being a realist. Some people can look at evidence, no matter how compelling, without being able to draw the obvious conclusion. Many politicians, for example, continue to insist that the way to improve education is to spend more despite the fact that since the 1970s, federal spending on education has nearly tripled, "while at the same time achievement has stagnated and graduation rates have hardly budged."[2] These politicians bring to mind Albert Einstein's definition of *insanity*: doing the same thing over and over again and expecting different results.

An important part of realism is acknowledging that actions have consequences. Without such an acknowledgment, one's view of reality becomes distorted. Nobel laureate Milton Friedman was being realistic when he said, "Nobody spends somebody else's money as carefully as he spends his own. Nobody uses somebody else's resources as carefully as he uses his own." But politicians are seemingly immune to realism. They spend money as if the bill will never come due. But it will; it always does.

Into each life a little reality must fall, though. And we, as citizens, get a chance every election day to impose some reality on our political leaders.

As much as some of us might not like the reality in which we find ourselves, simply wishing it away or, in the case of government overspending, ignoring it won't change things. Abraham Lincoln once asked, "How many legs does a dog have if you call the tail a leg? Four. Calling a tail a leg doesn't make it a leg." And calling huge increases in government spending "investment," as President Obama tends to do, doesn't change the fact that America currently faces a crushing overspending crisis. But our current president is far from the only politician who uses words not to illuminate reality, but to obscure it.

Changing Reality

Being a dreamer is an admirable quality, but once someone latches onto a dream it takes more than dreaming to make it a reality. Ambitious individuals with a dream, with an idea, require the know-how to set in motion the pieces to make that dream happen. Often dreamers get caught up in their dreams and lose the ability to think outside themselves, to think practically about what they're trying to accomplish. Only when they seek financing does reality come into play.

When someone is asked to risk the capital she has earned to support someone else's idea, that's often when reality creeps into the dreamer's head for the first time. While the dreamer assumes his idea will be the next iPod or microwave, the venture capitalist is the realist. Is the product viable? Is there a need? Is there a profit to be made?

The dreamers may not like what they hear, but sometimes it is difficult, if not impossible, to see the forest for the trees.

Being told an idea you are sure is a winner won't work is one of the most difficult things for anyone to hear, and history is full of people who were unable to acknowledge the unreality of their dreams and ended up ruined financially. It is also filled with those who were told their idea wasn't workable but succeeded in proving their critics wrong.

There's a fine line between genius and insanity, and sometimes it's difficult to figure out who is the dreamer and who is the realist. But for an individual to be successful, to change the way things are, he must somehow manage to be both a dreamer and a realist and to bring those seemingly contradictory characteristics to bear in all his undertakings.

Changing reality requires drive, determination, and most important, an accurate assessment of current conditions. Americans lead the world in innovation; industrial, scientific, and medical discoveries; and the creation of new products. Each of these started with a dream, but each was propelled forward by a keen sense of realism.

Idealistic Realism

The American Spirit is alive and well in our dreams, and it is rooted in what can ultimately be called *idealistic realism*. Consider some examples:

- American idealism: in 1776, the Founders issued a Declaration of Independence laying out our nation's core ideals. American realism: in 1789, the Founders produced the world's first written Constitution, creating the enduring institutions through which we realize our ideals.

- American idealism: America's foreign policy recognizes a responsibility to advance freedom around the world. American realism: the fundamental responsibility of American foreign policy is to ensure that America remains independent and protects its own vital national interests.

- American idealism: Lincoln issues the Emancipation Proclamation. American realism: he applies it only in areas under rebellion until after the Union has won the Civil War. Then, the realists make the idealists' dream a reality with the Thirteenth, Fourteenth, and Fifteenth Amendments to the Constitution.

- American idealism: we embrace immigrants from all over the world. American realism: we require everyone to integrate into the United States, speak English, and learn our history (or at least we used to).

- American idealism: when tragedy strikes, the president leads the country in prayer. American realism: we roll up our sleeves and get to work cleaning up and responding to the disaster.

- American idealism: a father dreams that his children will do better than he has in life. American realism: he works hard to provide opportunities for his children.

- American idealism: Americans start businesses, dreaming of success. American realism: we often fail, yet understand that it sometimes takes many tries to be successful, so we get right back up and try again.

And then there are the unsung heroes of American life, idealistic realists who know the worst about their fellow men, yet are inspired by their faith to devote their lives to helping them. Such a person is Bob Woodson, founder and president of the Center for Neighborhood Enterprise, which has offered support and training to more than two thousand grassroots leaders since 1981. He dubs these community servants "Josephs," counterparts to the biblical figure who guided Pharaoh through dangers by planning ahead and ended up providing for Israel too. Woodson wrote,

> The answers to many problems America faces can be found in our own modern-day Josephs. Many of these community healers have come out of our prisons. They have experienced what it is to live in drug-infested, crime-ridden neighborhoods. Many have, themselves, fallen but have been able to recover through their faith in God. Their authority is attested to, not by their position and prestige in society, but by the thousands of lives they have been able to reach and change. . . . They embrace the worst cases and they work with meager resources, yet their effectiveness eclipses that of conventional professional remedies. . . . The undeniable fact that lives have been transformed through the work of modern-day Josephs must be appreciated even by observers who may be skeptical about their approach.[3]

Every individual is different, with different ideas, abilities, and passions. The recognition of our true strengths allows us to make the most of them. Idealistic realists are honest about both their strengths and their weaknesses; they are inspired by great goals and lofty principles; and they are realistic about the means they use to achieve their goals. They truly embody the American Spirit at its best.

CHAPTER 14

Pragmatism

Failure is the opportunity to begin again more intelligently.

—Henry Ford

Pragmatism

Americans have won more Nobel Prizes, invented more products, written more books, and achieved a higher standard of living than virtually every other people on earth. Why? In part, it's because of the typically American characteristic known as pragmatism. We are a nation of pragmatic problem solvers, and whenever we're presented with an unorthodox solution to a problem that has baffled conventional thinkers, the first question we ask is: *Does it work?* If it does and if it's ethical, Americans press forward, following boldly in the footsteps of Civil War admiral David Farragut, who famously said, "Damn the torpedoes. Full speed ahead."[1]

To appreciate the important role that pragmatism has played in American history, you must first understand what pragmatism means—not as an abstract, academic philosophy, but as a challenging and demanding way of life. To be pragmatic, you must be humble enough, big enough, and honest enough to acknowledge three essential truths again and again:

1. **I was wrong.** If the situation has changed, and you have new information, or have changed your mind for any reason, be willing to admit you were wrong. Since you are going to be wrong again and again, the sooner you admit you are wrong and get on with the rest of your life, the better it will be for you and for everyone around you.

2. **I made a mistake.** You are not perfect. You do not have perfect knowledge. The more things you try, the more mistakes you will make. Successful people are not people who have never failed. Successful people fail, often as much or more than unsuccessful people. But they are not afraid to fail because they learn something every single time. If you have made a mistake, instead of bluffing, blustering, and trying to cover it up, admit it frankly and openly and get busy solving the problem or doing something else.

3. **I changed my mind.** It is amazing how many people make themselves emotionally and physically ill because of their unwillingness to admit that, with new information, they have changed their minds. People start businesses they shouldn't get into because they don't

want to admit they've changed their minds. People buy the wrong house or car because they don't want to admit they've changed their minds, and they end up with unaffordable monthly payments. It's a mark of courage and character, in a time of rapid and unpredictable change, to admit that you have changed your mind.

To be a pragmatist, you must be committed to your goal, but flexible in how you go about achieving it. Above all, you must be open to the possibility that your current course of action is completely wrong. As the nineteenth-century American newspaper publisher James Gordon Bennett observed, "I have made mistakes, but I never made the mistake of claiming that I never made one."[2]

Something Had to Be Done

The year 1776 was not a very good one for George Washington. His troops suffered a series of defeats on the battlefield and endured a long retreat through New Jersey after having to abandon New York City to British control. The setbacks left the morale of his troops low. Many were sick and underclothed. By December he was facing a dilemma: a significant portion of his troops would be eligible to go home at the end of the year, which would further deplete his forces. Washington's approach, up to that point, hadn't been working on any level. Something needed to be done; something had to change.

The first of Thomas Paine's pamphlet series *The American*

Crisis had just been published, so the general ordered it be read to the troops. It begins:

> THESE are the times that try men's souls. The summer soldier and the sunshine patriot will, in this crisis, shrink from the service of their country; but he that stands it now, deserves the love and thanks of man and woman. Tyranny, like hell, is not easily conquered; yet we have this consolation with us, that the harder the conflict, the more glorious the triumph. What we obtain too cheap, we esteem too lightly: it is dearness only that gives every thing its value. Heaven knows how to put a proper price upon its goods; and it would be strange indeed if so celestial an article as FREEDOM should not be highly rated. Britain, with an army to enforce her tyranny, has declared that she has a right (not only to TAX) but "to BIND us in ALL CASES WHATSOEVER," and if being bound in that manner, is not slavery, then is there not such a thing as slavery upon earth. Even the expression is impious; for so unlimited a power can belong only to God.[4]

Paine's inspiring words did lift morale, but not enough for General Washington. He needed something more. While camped for the winter near McKonkey's Ferry, Pennsylvania, Washington wrote, "I think the game is pretty near up."

With superior numbers and momentum on their side, the British and their feared Hessian mercenaries set up camp for the winter across the Delaware River, poised to resume their pursuit when the weather allowed. The Hessian troops were particularly fierce and known for their skills on the battlefield. Things were not looking good for the Americans. But Washington had an ace up his sleeve—his willingness to admit that his current plan wasn't working and to change it.

Washington, who had spent the previous few months on the defensive, decided it was now or never. He devised a plan for a surprise attack on Trenton, New Jersey, where the dreaded Hessians were camped. The Americans were low on supplies and facing weather and morale issues. This was really an all-or-nothing venture for them. On Christmas Day, only a week before the enlistments of many of his soldiers would end, Washington led his troops across the icy Delaware River into New Jersey. The element of surprise was on their side, and it was key. Washington led his troops into the Hessian camp, caught them off guard, and scored his victory. The Americans suffered minimal casualties—three dead, six wounded—and took a thousand prisoners.[4]

More important, Washington's gambit to change his fate worked. A full 50 percent of his soldiers reenlisted, saving the American army and the Revolution from collapse.[5] Morale rose significantly among the colonists as word of Washington's stunning victory spread across the land. It turned the tide and ended the first year of the war on a positive note, thus enabling the Americans to continue their struggle.

Building a Movement

In the early 1950s, American conservatism was in disarray. The distinguished liberal literary critic Lionel Trilling dismissed it as little more than a series of "irritable mental gestures which seem to resemble ideas."[6] But a brilliant Yale graduate named William F. Buckley Jr. was determined to unite the feuding conservative factions around a new magazine: *National Review*. Amazingly Buckley succeeded "by pointing out" (as *National Review*'s publisher, William A. Rusher, put it) "that they all had the same enemy—the liberals."[7]

Buckley recognized that the loose way in which American conservatism was structured just wasn't working. His unique genius as a fusionist lay in uniting disputatious traditionalists and libertarians into a modern conservative movement built around 4 core principles. Heritage scholar Lee Edwards summarized them as follows:

1. "It is not enough to be philosophically right. . . . You must also be technologically proficient. Conservatives must be expert in such tools of politics as precinct organization, communications, canvassing, direct mail, and polling."

2. "Conservatives must work together. There is not only safety but also strength in numbers."

3. "Conservatives should be realistic in their goals and patient in their realization. Like the Fabians in Great Britain and the progressives in America, conservatives must prepare themselves for a long march."

4. "Conservatives should be prudently optimistic, trusting in the ultimate good sense of the American people to make the right political decisions if given the right information."[8]

Buckley inherited a fortune and might easily have become, as Edwards put it, "the playboy of the Western world." Instead, he chose to become the Saint Paul of the modern American conservative movement: "His vision of ordered liberty shaped and molded and guided American conservatism from its infancy to its maturity, from a cramped suite of offices on Manhattan's East Side to the Oval Office of the White House, from a set of 'irritable mental gestures' to a political force that transformed American politics."[9]

Buckley sought out a handful of strong-minded, mutually antagonistic individualists and patiently fused them into the editorial board of *National Review*—one of America's finest political journals and the intellectual seedbed of today's conservative movement. His career exemplifies pragmatic intellectual leadership at its very best.

Personal Pragmatism

You don't have to fight in a war or build a political movement to practice pragmatism. Americans practice it in their personal lives every day.

Many, perhaps a majority, of your decisions, especially in your business and your career, will turn out to be wrong in the fullness of time.[10] This usually happens because the situation you're facing changes in some way after you make the decision, forcing you to reevaluate. Military planners often say that no battle plan survives contact with the enemy, and that is true. In today's fast-paced world, we receive new information constantly and must evaluate our decisions just as often.

There's nothing wrong with making a mistake or a bad decision as long as you are willing to admit it and change course or try something else.

As a pragmatist, you practice zero-based thinking regularly in every area of your life. You ask the question, *Is there anything I am doing today that, knowing what I now know, I wouldn't get into again if I had to do it over?* This is called a "KWINK Analysis"—knowing what I now know. Whenever you experience resistance, stress, frustration, or prolonged unhappiness about some situation in your life, be pragmatic and conduct a KWINK Analysis. Your only questions should be *Can it work?* and *Is it working?* If you would not get into the situation again today, as a pragmatist, be willing to cut your losses. Admit your mistake, and be willing to try something else. Management specialist Benjamin Tregoe said, "The very worst use of time is to do something very well that need not be done at all."

Parents practice pragmatism all the time. If a child exhibits an aptitude for sports, music, or acting, most parents will nurture that skill set—but not at the expense of schoolwork. The dream may be for those skills to lead to a long, successful career in those highly competitive fields. But the practical-thinking parent realizes that the odds of success are long. To paraphrase the old proverb, they hope for the best but prepare (their children) for the rest.

The same goes for the nation as a whole. In times of tragedy, such as a hurricane or after 9/11, Americans, led by the president, pray for the victims and the survivors, but people know that is not enough. After the prayers, Americans roll up their sleeves and get to work cleaning up and volunteering to help those in need. After Hurricane Katrina, Americans across the country opened their homes to families who had lost everything. At the same time hundreds of thousands went to the Gulf coast to help clean up and rebuild. The idealism and spirit-lifting nature of the prayers were exactly what were needed at that moment, and the practical nature of the follow-up helping hands took prayers to action and physically improved lives.

America is the land of unlimited opportunities. At any time you can draw a line through your past and start again. In America you can reinvent yourself on a regular basis, and you should do so. Imagine starting your business or career over again today. What would you do differently? What would be the first things you would start up again? What would you discontinue altogether? Imagine you are a scriptwriter in Hollywood, and no one wants to buy the script for your new movie. Remember, you can tear up your current script and write a new one, starting now. Nothing holds you back but yourself.

Pragmatism Under Assault

Of course, as the role of government in our society increases, this fortunate situation may well change. Americans are likely to encounter new and unexpected obstacles to their advancement, should government ever become the principal arbiter of our destinies. It is to be hoped, however, that no American ever faces the kinds of roadblocks that Winston Churchill encountered in the 1930s as he sought to alert his British countrymen to the growing Nazi peril. As Milton Friedman has reminded us:

From 1933 to the outbreak of World War II, Churchill was not permitted to talk over the British radio, which was, of course, a government monopoly administered by the British Broadcasting Corporation. Here was a leading citizen of his country, a Member of Parliament, a former cabinet minister, a man who was desperately trying by every device to persuade his countrymen to take steps to ward off the menace of Hitler's Germany. He was not permitted to talk over the radio to the British people, because the BBC was a government monopoly and his position was too "controversial."[11]

Today, America faces new threats not from Nazism or communism, but from radical Islamists bent on our destruction. These threats call for a pragmatic response, yet from President Obama on down, many Americans are reluctant even to *identify* radical Islamist ideology as a major danger to Americans for fear that they might be mistaken for anti-Muslim bigots. Social critic Bruce Bawer wrote about this issue:

Americans are, or used to be, a pragmatic people. They were never, in considerable numbers, captives of *any* fact-defying ideology. What mattered was the testimony of their senses; what mattered was getting things done, making things better, solving problems, figuring out what worked and what didn't. Whether they called themselves liberals or conservatives mattered infinitely less than the fact that they shared this sensible, practical, eyes-wide-open approach to the world. But today the ideological malady that afflicted the most extreme of 1960s radicals has infected millions of rank-and-file Democrats. The refusal to acknowledge the facts on the ground because they conflict with political correctness, with multiculturalism, with orthodox New Left ideology, is a phenomenon that has deep roots but that came into full bloom only after 9/11.[12]

Americans have never shied away from controversy. On the contrary, we thrive on it. Being outspoken, taking a stand, daring to be unconventional, trying, failing, learning from our mistakes, and starting all over again are quintessential features of the American Spirit. But pragmatism and political correctness rarely go hand in hand, and when political correctness trumps pragmatism—as it did in Great Britain during the 1930s and as it threatens to do in the United States today—the results are likely to be catastrophic.

CHAPTER 15

Problem Solving

We can't solve problems by using the same kind of thinking
we used when we created them.

—Albert Einstein

Problem Solving

Americans are intensely solution oriented. We chew up problems
and spit them out. As far as Americans are concerned, a problem
is merely a challenge, something to rise to. Americans are among
the greatest problem solvers on earth, unstoppable in every field,
from opening up a vast continent to exploring outer space.

"An inventor is a man who looks upon the world and is not
contented with things as they are. He wants to improve whatever he sees; he wants to benefit the world," Alexander Graham
Bell explained.

Americans drink up problems that have stopped and stumped

others. There are no problems that cannot be solved; it is only a matter of *how* or how long until hitherto unrevealed information can be brought to bear on seemingly insoluble problems. "There are no big problems; there are just lots of little problems," Henry Ford believed.

The most successful Americans are the great problem solvers of business, science, technology, religion, medicine, government, military operations, and day-to-day life. Problem solving is a part of our heritage. It is in the American DNA.

Finding Cures

There is perhaps nothing more frightening than disease. Diseases strike indiscriminately, with no warning.

The plague of the twentieth century was called poliomyelitis, or polio. It was an untreatable virus that attacked mostly children, destroying muscles and causing paralysis. Tens of thousands of children were stricken, disabled by this dreaded disease. It seemed to strike randomly and without mercy or warning.

Polio had been around for centuries in small pockets and outbreaks around the world, but in the late nineteenth century it began to reach epidemic levels. Outbreaks occurred with greater frequency and severity. With parents living in fear of their children contracting the disease, governments and labs directed resources toward finding a vaccine.

After years of failure, Dr. Jonas Salk at the University of Pittsburgh struck gold in 1955. He hadn't created a cure for polio; Americans haven't created a cure for viral diseases yet, but Salk had developed a vaccine that would prevent any more children from succumbing to this invisible monster.

When Salk's discovery was tested and proven successful, it made news around the world. Parents breathed a sigh of relief as their children were immunized. It is estimated that by the year 2005 some five hundred million children had been immunized.

Although it is not 100 percent effective, the result of Salk's work has been monumental. In addition to the direct and immediate impact of Salk's discovery, it inspired others to follow in his footsteps and find more cures and treatments. Getting AIDS was once a death sentence; thanks to scientists, pharmaceutical companies, and innovation, it has now become a manageable illness.

While some may insist that such improvements should be encouraged only if they are not financially remunerative, allowing pharmaceutical companies and inventors to reap financial rewards from their work will encourage more lifesaving work, making everyone better off. It is hard to imagine an industry so demonized that has done so much to make life better for so many—investors, inventors, and everyday people, a.k.a. consumers.

A Revolutionary Problem

The fact that our Founding Fathers were brilliant men is beyond debate, but they were not perfect. Once the Revolutionary War was won, they needed to form a government. But what type?

During the war the Founders drafted the Articles of Confederation and Perpetual Union, designed to loosely bind the states together and ensure peace and harmony among them after the war. It was finally ratified by the states in 1781 and became the law of the land. When the war ended in 1783, the Articles of Confederation were the contract by which the states cooperated, but the governing body it created had very little power. The Articles soon proved to be insufficient to hold the Union together.

In 1787 a new Constitutional Convention was called in Philadelphia to revise the Articles of Confederation and address the document's shortcomings. Instead of amending the weak Articles, the delegates decided to begin anew, to form a national government that would, from the start, address the issues the Articles didn't, as well as any other problems they could foresee. It was a risky endeavor that went well beyond the mission with which their respective states had charged them.

They knew the weaknesses of the Articles and did their best to address them in what became the Constitution of the United States. More than that, they had the foresight to recognize that nothing they could come up with would be perfect, so they created a mechanism by which the document could be amended to address situations as they arose.

They knew that perfection was reserved for God, so they did not strive for that. In the preamble to the Constitution they stated clearly that their objective was to "form a more perfect Union," and in that document they moved further toward perfection than any government had before or since.

Not everyone was happy with the Constitution. In fact, no one was completely happy with it. Rhode Island, for example, refused to send a representative to the convention. But the state had the wisdom to see the convention had addressed the problems in the Articles of Confederation and created a government with which they could all live and flourish. Benjamin Franklin, perhaps the most respected member of the Constitutional Convention, wasn't completely satisfied either, but helped steer the convention to approve the Constitution so it could be sent to the states for ratification. He knew it was the best that they as human beings could do. He said, "There are several parts of this Constitution which I do not at present approve, but I am not sure I shall never approve them. . . . I doubt too whether any other Convention we can obtain, may be able to make a better Constitution. . . . It therefore astonishes me, Sir, to find this system approaching so near to perfection as it does; and I think it will astonish our enemies."[1]

It did. It was sent to the states for their approval, and of course it was approved. On March 4, 1789, the government created by the Constitution came into existence and has been working ever since. The Founding Fathers had successfully identified and addressed the problems in the Articles of Confederation and had moved the United States government closer to perfection. But their task remains uncompleted, and it remains for us—and for those who will come after us—to make it "more perfect" still.

Everyday Problems

Not every problem is on such a grand scale or requires a grand solution. Some are a simple matter of basic humanity. But they must be risen to as well.

Western Oregon and Central Washington were neck and neck in the NCAA Division II softball conference standings. Western Oregon needed a win in the afternoon game of their doubleheader, and Sara Tucholsky was happy to be in their lineup for what could be the final collegiate softball game of her career.

The senior outfielder was never a force to be reckoned with at the plate, but she loved to play the game. After thousands of at bats Sara stepped into the batter's box and ended a 0–0 tie with the first home run of her career. As she rounded first base with a grin that could be seen clear across the stadium, something went wrong. She dropped to the ground and could not stand up. She would find out later that she tore her anterior cruciate ligament (ACL). Lying there on the dirt, all she could think about was the trot around bases that she would never finish. Her coach tried to find a way that she could substitute a player to run the bases for Sara and still give her the credit for her first home run. But the umpires stated very clearly that it was against the rules. When it seemed inevitable that Sara would have to settle for just another single, an incredible young lady stepped forward and offered a solution.

Central Washington senior Mallory Holtman owned almost every hitting record you could think of from her school and the conference. For Mallory, itting home runs was as commonplace as waking up every morning. After watching the jubilation that Sara displayed as she came out of the batter's box with her first home run and the devastation as she lay in a heap on the infield dirt, Mallory knew something must be done. So after conferring with a nearby teammate she walked over to the umpires and asked, "Excuse me, would it be OK if we carried her around and she touched each bag?" The umpires looked at each other and nodded. They said that would be within the rules and would allow Sara to realize her dream of finishing her home run trot. The crowd went wild as the opposing teammates picked her up and gingerly lowered her foot on each base and ultimately home plate.

Mallory's act gave Western Oregon the lead in the game and in the end caused her own team to lose the game and the conference championship. But Mallory wouldn't change a thing knowing what she knows now, that her season would end a few games early because of what she did. She says, "It was the right thing to do. She hit the ball over the fence, she deserved a home run." Her quick thinking and problem-solving good nature did not go unnoticed. She was honored with ESPN's Espy for "Best Sports Moment of the Year." Mallory Holtman is an outstanding example of the American Spirit.

Life Without Problems?

Problems are the stepping-stones to success. They are to be welcomed, not avoided. You actually rise in life, in responsibilities and rewards, to the degree to which you can solve problems.

But will we Americans always be a nation of problem solvers? Will we always enjoy the unique satisfactions that problem solving brings? Nearly 180 years ago, Alexis de Tocqueville, a young French aristocrat visiting America for the first time, issued a dire warning. All democracies, Tocqueville declared— even the young and strapping American democracy—have a tendency to succumb to a centralized form of government that promises to solve every problem, but in the process saps its citizens of their courage and robs them of their spirit:

Above [the people] an immense tutelary power is elevated, which alone takes charge of assuring their enjoyments and watching over their fate. It is absolute, detailed, regular, far-seeing, and mild. It would resemble paternal power if, like that, it had for its object to prepare men for manhood; but on the contrary, it seeks only to keep them fixed irrevocably in childhood; it likes its citizens to enjoy themselves provided that they think only of enjoying themselves. It willingly works for their happiness; but it wants to be the sole agent and sole arbiter of that; it provides for their security, foresees and secures their needs, facilitates their pleasures, conducts their principal affairs, directs their industry, regulates their estates, divides their inheritances: can it not take away from them entirely the trouble of thinking and the pain of living?[2]

Americans must never succumb to such an "immense tutelary power" that reduces us to "nothing more than a herd of timid and industrious animals of which the government is the shepherd." Such a "soft despotism" would provide us with cradle-to-grave security, but at the cost of our humanity. As social scientist Charles Murray has written, "Responsibility is what keeps our lives from becoming trivial."[3]

Problem solving makes us stronger, smarter, and more confident. It also brings out the best in people, as in the case of Mallory Holtman. Without both the ability and the responsibility to solve the problems we encounter on a regular basis, neither success nor happiness is possible.

Historically Americans have risen to every challenge we have faced and have seen opportunities in every problem we have encountered. But the ambition of the modern welfare state is to eliminate problems entirely and provide a government guarantee of security for all. Social critic Jonah Goldberg observed, "The real threat is that the promise of American life will be frittered away for a bag of magic beans called security. . . . Many progressives seem to think that we can transform America into a vast college campus where food, shelter, and recreation are all provided for us and the only crime is to be mean to somebody else, particularly a minority."[4]

Such a problem-free state of affairs, should it ever come to pass, would not only affect domestic policy. The ramifications of the welfare-state mentality extend to foreign policy as well. Irving Kristol declared,

> The fully developed welfare state is a modern version of the feudal castle, guarded by moats and barriers, and offering security and shelter to the loyal population that gathers around it. Ironically, this means that in world affairs the poorer nations that are not welfare states, and are not nearly as risk-averse since they have so little to lose, will be (as they are already becoming) the activist countries, the ones that create the crises and set the international agenda. The most powerful nations in the world—economically, technologically, even militarily—will become citadels of resistance and nothing more.[5]

Is the United States destined to become nothing more than a "citadel of resistance" to the crimes and outrages of rogue states and terrorist networks? Or will a vigorous and self-confident

United States continue to set the political, economic, and intellectual agendas for the rest of mankind in the twenty-first century, just as it has in the twentieth century? Much depends on the strength of the American Spirit and on the refusal of ordinary Americans to be seduced by the false promise of the welfare state: a secure, affluent, and problem-free existence.

CHAPTER 16

Generosity

Philanthropy is almost the only virtue which is sufficiently
appreciated by mankind.

—Henry David Thoreau

Generosity

Americans overall are the most generous people on earth and in
all human history.

Although the American economy is responsible for a little
more than one-fifth of the world's total GDP, Americans give
more in charity to the less fortunate than the rest of the world
put together. We donated more than $300 billion in 2009, despite
the economic downturn. This number represents private giving
from individuals and organizations, offered voluntarily, out of
the goodness of their hearts.

Americans give money out of their pockets to support charities, churches, schools, universities, and many thousands of nonprofit organizations that work for the betterment of society. We remember that "generosity is a reflection of what one does with his or her own resources and not what he or she advocates the government do with everyone's money," as Ronald Reagan explained.

In addition, individual Americans contribute millions of hours of their time each year to help and support people and causes, working out to an average of three hours per week per person. Americans give more of themselves and their personal income to assist the less fortunate than all other nations on a per person basis. Truly, we heed George Washington's call: "Let your heart feel for the afflictions and distresses of everyone, and let your hand give in proportion to your purse, remembering . . . that it is not everyone who asketh that deserveth charity."[1]

The biggest supporters of the less fortunate are often the beneficiaries of successful businesses, both past and present. American fortunes funded the billions of dollars in the Ford, Carnegie, Mellon, Nobel, Scaife, and Rockefeller foundations, among others. Today, the Bill and Melinda Gates Foundation, bolstered by the fortune of Warren Buffett, has created a $52 billion charity to help people all over America and the world.

Disaster Relief

When natural disasters strike, Americans rally around the flag like no other people on earth. After the devastation caused by Hurricane Katrina along the coast of the Gulf of Mexico, Americans donated more than $3 billion to rebuild and aid those who lost everything in the storm.[2] These donations were made even though people understood the federal government would allocate some 62.3 billion tax dollars to the effort.[3]

But Americans' generosity knows no boundaries and doesn't stop at our nation's borders. Whenever and wherever disaster strikes, Americans are there to help without question. In addition to the military and financial donations our government makes, Americans reach deep into their own pockets when their fellow human beings are in need. After the tragic tsunami hit the Indian Ocean in 2004, killing more than 230,000 and rendering millions homeless, Americans donated more than $3.16 billion to help rebuild those lives destroyed.[4] And in the days after the disaster, it was the American navy (with some help from our Australian and British allies) that got water plants running and delivered emergency aid.

After an earthquake devastated the Haitian capital of Port-au-Prince, killing more than 200,000 and leaving more than 1.5 million people homeless in 2010, Americans donated $1.3 billion from their own pockets to help rebuild the devastated island nation.[5] Of this, 25 percent of American households contributed to the relief, totaling $2.78 billion in donations, $340 million came from corporations, and $40 million came from foundations. The largest percentage of donors (37 percent) reported making donations through their places of worship.[6] The generosity of the American people doesn't decrease because of poor economic circumstances at home. For example, the donations to the Haitian relief efforts were made at the height of a major recession in the United States.

Americans have donated billions of dollars in relief funds to aid every natural disaster relief effort around the globe, even when that nation's government is our adversary. The American people provided $74 million in the first year following Cyclone Nargis to Myanmar, where the government remains hostile to America.[7]

"Private charities, as well as contributions to public purposes in proportion to every one's circumstances, are certainly among the duties we owe to society," Thomas Jefferson explained, and Americans have been living up to that creed ever since.

The Marshall Plan

We draw a sharp distinction between the charitable actions of private individuals and government programs designed to help the less fortunate. The former are freely made decisions that reflect deeply held personal values; the latter are the result of decisions made by politicians and bureaucrats, are imposed on taxpayers, and often end up crowding out private charity, undermining personal initiative, creating a culture of dependency, and—in the case of foreign aid—propping up corrupt dictatorships and self-interested elites.

But not all government-run programs are counterproductive. Perhaps the most successful act of government generosity in all history was the European Recovery Plan, commonly referred to as the Marshall Plan, named after American secretary of state George Marshall.

The Marshall Plan helped fend off the encroaching threat of communism in the devastated nations of post–World War II Western Europe. Fearing that widespread poverty in Western Europe threatened to bring Communist parties to power, Secretary Marshall laid out his plan in a commencement address at Harvard University in 1947. "The truth of the matter is that Europe's requirements for the next three or four years of foreign food and other essential products—principally from America—are so much greater than her present ability to pay that she must have substantial additional help or face economic, social, and political deterioration of a very grave character," he said.

The plan cost $14.607 billion, which was on top of the $8.962 billion the United States had spent aiding Europe since the end of the war. This $23.569 billion was 10 percent of America's 1947 GDP. Government generosity on such a colossal scale was truly unprecedented. Moreover, no one knew for certain whether the Marshall Plan would actually succeed in jump-starting Western Europe's stalled economies. But the gamble paid off, and America's generosity was rewarded. By the end of the rebuilding in 1952, the threat from the growing Communist influence had subsided as the economies of the participating countries recovered to prewar levels. And they continued to expand.

Both the United States and the nations of Western Europe benefited immensely from the Marshall Plan—a rare example of government generosity that accomplished its purpose and helped secure freedom and prosperity in a strategically vital part of the world.

Selflessness

Generosity takes many forms, everything from volunteering your time at a soup kitchen to buying a homeless man a sandwich when you see him outside a store. Not all of it is registered in the total giving of the country, but all of it helps. And not all forms of charity require a monetary transaction; some are simply generous acts of selflessness.

Ronald Griffin was a fifty-eight-year-old suffering from congestive heart failure. Dennis Korzelius was a forty-three-year-old suffering from cirrhosis of the liver. Antwan Hunter was a sixteen-year-old suffering from kidney failure. David Erving was a forty-year-old suffering from diabetes. All four had been told that if a miracle transplant didn't become available almost immediately, they would die.

Jason Ray could not have been farther from death's door. He was a larger-than-life twenty-one-year-old with a promising future. A die-hard University of North Carolina Tar Heel, he had been the official mascot of UNC for three years and was traveling with the men's basketball team to their Sweet Sixteen match-up with the University of Southern California one March. After what Jason was sure would be a national championship season for the Tar Heels, he would be graduating and already had a job lined up. He was enjoying his last few weeks as Rameses, the lifeblood and spirit of UNC.

That Friday night Jason decided to walk to the nearest gas station to grab a burrito and soda before the game. As he walked along Route 4 to the Fort Lee Hilton in his Tar Heel sweats, he was struck by a reckless driver. His parents held out hope until they arrived at the hospital in New Jersey and looked at their son, lying almost lifeless. Later that night Jason was pronounced dead, but not before his parents signed the papers to donate his organs, a decision Jason had made a few years back that, at the time, both his mom and dad disapproved.

Jason gave Ronald his heart, Dennis his liver, Antwan his kidney, and David his pancreas and kidney. All four survived and eventually were able to meet Emmitt and Charlotte Ray in an emotional afternoon that began and ended with hugs, tears, and an immeasurable amount of gratitude for a twenty-one-year-old's selfless gift.

Because of Jason's generosity, five children have their fathers back. Four mothers have their sons back. As many as seventy-five others benefited from tissue donation, such as a new cornea or a new ACL. But just as important, two parents from North Carolina started to find peace with the tragedy that shook their world not long ago.

"Forget the fact that Jason was my son," Emmitt says. "Every time I turn around, I learn more and more about the effect he had on this world. And as time goes by, I realize how lucky I was to have even known such a man."

Benefiting the Giver

In *Poor Richard's Almanack*, Benjamin Franklin asserted, "When you are good to others, you are best to yourself."[8] That charity, given for the right reasons and in the right way, benefits the receiver is obvious; that it also benefits the giver, as Franklin maintained, is less obvious, but equally true. Heritage scholar Dr. Ryan Messmore wrote,

> Giving our time and money to others tends to have significant implications for our individual well-being and that of our local communities and nation. Charitable giving is associated

with higher levels of health and happiness, increased prosperity and strong community organizations. . . .

Without charity, Americans would become more dependent on impersonal government for a vast array of services. This, in turn, would foster a social relationship where one side perceives aid as a forced penalty rather than a voluntary offering and the other side views aid as a right rather than a gift.

Impersonal government checks can foster a mentality that undercuts the motivation to feel or give gratitude when received. In contrast, gifts create a kind of momentum of good will, which has the potential to bind both giver and receiver into a more personal relationship.[9]

Undermining Generosity

A wise government will therefore enact policies that clear the way for citizens to act generously and will refrain from placing obstacles in the way of their generosity. Unfortunately the Obama administration has consistently sought to undermine charitable giving in the United States. The president's fiscal year 2012 budget proposal, for example, raises the tax rate on upper-income individuals and families and reduces their income tax deductions for charitable donations. These two tax code changes will discourage charitable donations and leave the most generous donors with less money to donate. They will shift resources from private nonprofit charitable organizations to the federal government, which is consistently less effective in caring for needy people.

Nor is this the first time President Obama has sought to

use changes in the tax code to reduce charitable giving. As Dr. Messmore noted:

Obama made a similar attempt to reduce charitable deductions in his Fiscal Year 2010 budget. During that debate, scholars at the Center on Philanthropy at Indiana University estimated that Obama's proposed changes would have reduced total itemized giving by wealthy households by almost $4 billion. While this is only a small percentage of total annual charitable donations, it is more than the combined annual operating budgets of the American Cancer Society, World Vision, St. Jude's Children's Research Hospital, Habitat for Humanity, and the American Heart Association. . . .

Regrettably, President Obama's proposed tax changes would move the dial of social responsibility one more notch in the direction of the state. This sets the stage for adopting future policies that could further chip away at local, personal and mutual obligations and increase dependence on government.[10]

Americans are the most generous people in all history. We are also the most blessed people in all history. Could these two facts somehow be related? Are we blessed *because* we are generous? All we can say for sure is that the generosity of ordinary Americans benefits them, their neighbors, and the world. It is a vital aspect of the American Spirit that government would be well advised to foster and must be careful never to undermine.

CHAPTER 17

Capitalism

Giving is the vital impulse and moral center of capitalism.

—George Gilder, American writer and activist

Over the past one hundred years few institutions have been attacked so fiercely, so falsely, and so foolishly as capitalism has been. Governments based on the idea that capitalism is evil, and that the state can create and control an entire economy, have risen and fallen during this period, but capitalism continues to thrive. Today, it is no longer beyond the pale to say that capitalism has done more good for more people than any other economic arrangement ever devised by man.

Capitalism in America

Capitalist economies like the United States are prosperous, growing, and expansive, creating opportunities and wealth for ever increasing numbers of people. "I think all the world would gain by setting commerce at perfect liberty," Thomas Jefferson said, and our Constitution was a major step in that direction. Capitalism is based on free markets, on the opportunities for anyone to enter any market at any time to produce and offer products and services that people want, need, and will purchase.

Capitalism is really *savings-ism*. Fixed capital consists of real estate, factories, machinery, equipment, airlines, railroads, telecommunications equipment, and all other factors of production that can be used to produce and distribute products and services to ever more people. Capital is accumulated only when people refrain from spending everything they earn, saving it instead, and reinvesting it to produce even more goods and services in the future.

For example, a farmer plants seeds, nurtures their sprouts, and harvests the crop in the fall. He then sells his crops to the highest bidder, but keeps back sufficient seed to replant and begin again in the spring. This unconsumed excess is a form of capital.

Businesses produce and sell products and services, earning income that is paid out for wages, salaries, machines, raw materials, and other expenses. Businesses hold back part of their income to reinvest in research and development and the production of new goods and services for the future.

If a farmer consumes all his seed corn, or a business spends all its income, it will have no future. The opposite of capitalism is subsistence and poverty, living from hand to mouth, never getting ahead.

America is great because it offers the opportunity for almost everyone to work, save, invest, and build capital over time. This accumulated capital can be used to start a business or can be combined with the capital of others to underwrite the creation of larger corporations. Stock markets represent a place where people can pool their capital and invest it in enterprises, along with the capital of others, to produce and sell products and services and earn profits and dividends, which are then distributed to the stockholders as the owners of the business.

Capitalism depends on a combination of productivity and self-discipline or self-denial. Capitalism requires the ability to delay gratification in the short term in order to enjoy greater rewards in the long term. It accepts, and helps tame, human nature. As editor, publisher, and businessman Steve Forbes observed in a 1998 lecture to the Heritage Foundation, capitalism "encourages ambitious individuals to engage in peaceful pursuits instead of plundering their neighbors. An entrepreneur offers something—a product or service. You do not have to accept it. It is a voluntary transaction. It encourages cooperation."[1]

America is great because it provides a legal and social framework consisting of clearly understood laws, legally sanctioned contracts, and a stable currency that creates sufficient security for people to save, invest, and risk their capital in the anticipation of achieving greater wealth in the future.

America is great because its capitalist system enables the average person to start with little and build a substantial estate over the course of a working lifetime. America has more millionaires and billionaires than all the other countries in the world. Fully 80 percent of wealthy Americans started at the bottom and earned their money in one generation as the result of starting and building capitalistic enterprises. As Steve Forbes put it:

> The Bible talks about how the last shall be first. That is certainly true in a spiritual sense. And with democratic capitalism, it is also true in a material sense. In a free enterprise economy, the least of us can constantly challenge the powerful and succeed in overthrowing the powerful. The last becomes first. We saw it with Robert Goizueta, a refugee from communist Cuba who eventually rose to be head of Coca-Cola and made it a fabulous success. You see it with so many others in our history—from Andrew Carnegie to Andrew Grove, a refugee from Hungary. My own grandfather, B. C. Forbes, the sixth of ten children, never got beyond the sixth grade, but founded a great enterprise. That is what the spirit of enterprise is all about.[2]

Where some nations have age-old caste systems or entrenched class systems from which escape to a better life is next to impossible, the free market capitalist system in the United States presents opportunities for every individual to improve his or her life.

America is great because America is free, and should we ever lose the economic freedom that capitalism secures, our political freedom will also be gravely threatened. Heritage scholars Kim Holmes and Matthew Spalding offered this example of what could happen:

> We only need recall the human toll of slavery and Soviet Communism to understand what Friedrich Hayek meant

when he noted that "to be controlled in our economic pursuits means to be always controlled," and that if all economic decisions require the approval of government, then "we should really be controlled in everything." In the end, liberty is whole and universal: The world will not be free politically if it is not free economically.[3]

The Entrepreneurial Spirit

Capitalism cannot exist without entrepreneurs—the men and women who take the risks and start the businesses that produce the goods and services we all enjoy. Almost every entrepreneurial business begins with one or two individuals, an idea, and a kitchen table. Microsoft began with two university students, Bill Gates and Paul Allen, and an idea to develop a software program they could sell to an emerging computer company. Sam Walton started Wal-Mart with a single store offering low-priced products in a small town in Arkansas. Many entrepreneurial companies and fortunes began with individuals selling single products or services out of their homes and going from door to door or office to office.

The key to entrepreneurial success is to find a need and fill it. This ability to define an unsatisfied need accurately and create a product or service people will buy, at a price they are willing to pay, is the key to successful entrepreneurial activity. As one of this book's authors observed, "It has been noted by conservatives that to prosper as a Socialist you need to threaten the people, but to prosper as a capitalist you need to please them."[4]

The entrepreneur is the spark plug in the free market

economy. The vision of providing a product or a service that people are willing to pay for, combined with the ability to produce that product or service at a cost below the market sales price, propels the entrepreneur into action. Giving people what they want, at prices they can afford, is the essence of capitalism.

Entrepreneurs undertake risk in the pursuit of profit. They have the marketable ability to bring together the various factors of production and combine them into a product or service that can be sold in a competitive market. In many ways this is an act of genius, requiring a special ability.

Each society depends on the activities and successes of entrepreneurs to drive it forward. Entrepreneurs create wealth, jobs, profits, and new opportunities. Entrepreneurial activity generates the tax revenues that pay for roads, hospitals, schools, national defense, and everything else our nation needs to survive and prosper. "Some people regard private enterprise as a predatory tiger to be shot. Others look on it as a cow they can milk. Not enough people see it as a healthy horse, pulling a sturdy wagon," Winston Churchill explained.

Small- and medium-size businesses, started by entrepreneurs, create 70 to 90 percent of all new jobs in America. While large companies have been laying off tens of thousands of people in recent years, small companies, sometimes just mom-and-pop operations, have been steadily hiring and growing.

Each year the World Bank produces the report "Doing Business." This report measures the ease of starting and building a business, taking into consideration laws, regulations, taxes, economic climate, distribution channels, and many other factors for more than 150 countries around the world.

According to this report, year after year, the United States is one of the easiest countries in the world in which to start a business, taking less than twenty-four hours from having a business idea to registering it online to engaging in actual business activities. In fact, in America you can decide to start a new business over lunch and be buying and selling products and services that afternoon, even before you think of a name or open a bank account.

Entrepreneurs believe and accept that the road to success is paved with hard work. Most self-made millionaires in America are entrepreneurs, founders of their own businesses, engaged with people who work with and for them. Eighty-five percent of successful entrepreneurs attribute their success to hard work. They start a little earlier, work a little harder, and stay a little later, often for many years, before they become successful. President Harry Truman observed, "I studied the lives of great men and famous women, and I found that the men and women who got to the top were those who did the jobs they had in hand, with everything they had of energy and enthusiasm and hard work."

Entrepreneurs are unafraid to take on responsibility. As one of this book's coauthors has written: "Entrepreneurs accept complete responsibility for themselves, for their companies, and for everything they do. Instead of making excuses, they make progress. They don't blame other people for their problems. They refuse to complain. They don't criticize or condemn. Instead, they say, 'I am responsible!' They take charge, and get on with the job."[5]

Americans are natural entrepreneurs. They constantly take risks and seek creative ways to buy, sell, and trade their work, products, or services at better prices.

The Amway Story

The American spirit of entrepreneurship is well illustrated by the phenomenal experience of Amway. This unique American success story enables more than three million people to own and operate independent businesses. These business owners enjoy wide discretion over their products, their employees, and their sales. Indeed, they enjoy as much control over their enterprises as any other independent business owners. They have one advantage: they draw from the experience and market-tested materials that have made Amway into a top global enterprise.

The history of this company provides an insight into the power of American entrepreneurship to transform the lives of millions. In 1959, Rich DeVos and Jay Van Andel founded Amway Corporation. Like most American business owners, they started small. Their first product was a dietary supplement, and they sold it door-to-door in their neighborhood, Grand Rapids, Michigan, trusting the word of mouth of satisfied customers. The key to a successful business, they discovered, is to cultivate personal relationships and trust. They expanded their business and developed Liquid Organic Cleaner, an environmentally friendly home care product still sold today.

The company expanded rapidly and over the next few years employed more than seven hundred people, sold more than two hundred products, and worked with more than one hundred thousand distributors. Amway's annual sales exceeded $500 million by the late 1960s.

With success now manifest at home, DeVos and Van Andel asked themselves, *Why not go out into the world?* New markets were expanding overseas—in Australia, the United Kingdom, Hong Kong, Malaysia, and Japan—and Amway quickly unlocked them.

A humanitarian benefit emerged from Amway's entrepreneurship. The company's original focus on health and nutrition inspired their researchers to develop a water treatment system, called e-Spring®, that would provide clean water to places around the world that desperately needed it.

DeVos and Van Andel had created a much-studied business model. People who shared their belief in entrepreneurship could share in the company's considerable success. By the mid-1970s, Amway was shipping products to millions of family-owned distributors. By the last decade of the last century, the company's sales exceeded $5 billion; the company now operates in eighty countries and territories around the world.

This American success story is not only the story of two talented entrepreneurs; it is also the story of the small businesses that made Amway's success possible. If not for the talents of millions of small business owners, Amway would never have thrived. Only in America can a business like Amway rightly claim to be the creation of millions of energetic entrepreneurs.

Failure

Entrepreneurship is risky. Fully 80 percent of entrepreneurial businesses fail or close down within the first two to four years. Of the 20 percent that survive, only 20 percent of those (thus 4 percent of the total) will go on to be significantly profitable. And of the 4 percent that survive, only 20 of those (0.8 percent) will go on to be medium-size and larger businesses generating millions of dollars in sales.

But while it may well seem that the opposite of success is failure, it really isn't so. Each failure offers an opportunity to learn and improve, a chance to find another path to success. No, the opposite of success is not failure; it's quitting. General Colin Powell said, "There are no secrets to success. It is the result of preparation, hard work, and learning from failure."

Some of the most successful entrepreneurs in history failed in their first attempts at success, and many failed several times. As novelist C. S. Lewis put it, "Failures are finger posts on the road to achievement."

Everyone knows about the Ford Motor Company and its founder, Henry Ford, but Henry Ford didn't start out as "Henry Ford." In 1899, Ford started the Detroit Automobile Company. Two years later it filed for bankruptcy. It wasn't until 1903 that Henry started Ford, which would eventually make him one of the richest men in the world. Were it not for that initial failure, Ford might not have become what he became. Had he quit, he definitely would not have. Oh, and don't feel bad for the Detroit Automobile Company; it eventually reorganized and emerged from bankruptcy (without Ford) as the Cadillac Automobile Company. Evidently it, too, learned from its mistakes.

But Henry Ford is far from alone on the list of success stories that could easily have gone the other way. The list of widely recognized names is long and illustrious, and it goes to prove what the great football coach Vince Lombardi said: "It's not whether you get knocked down; it's whether you get up."

Milton Hershey, founder of Hershey's Chocolate, had two

candy shops go bankrupt before finding sweet success. Walt Disney is famous the world over for his movies and theme parks, but his first venture into show business ended when his film company went belly-up in 1923. It wasn't until his next try five years later, and with a mouse character he created, that he found his key to the Magic Kingdom.

Baseball legend Mickey Mantle was sent down to the minor leagues after his first stint in the majors. He considered giving up because he wasn't sure he had what it took to be a big leaguer. When he expressed his doubts to his father, the senior Mantle drove to Kansas City, where his son had been sent, and started packing his clothes for him. When Mickey asked what he was doing, his father replied, "I thought I raised a man. I see I raised a coward instead. You can come back to Oklahoma and work the mines with me." Needless to say, Mickey changed his tune and his fortune, going on to become one of the most successful and beloved baseball players ever.

The list of successful people who have faced failure and/ or bankruptcy contains more names that we all recognize: Woolworth, Macy, Trump, Edison, Lincoln, and many, many more. Needless to say, there are very few people who've succeeded greatly who haven't, at one point or another, failed miserably, but none of them quit. They picked themselves up, dusted themselves off, and tried again. The words of the English folk song "Sir Andrew Barton" apply to virtually every successful entrepreneur:

> I am hurt but I am not slain.
> I'll lay me down and bleed awhile,
> Then I'll rise and fight again.[6]

Some people do not understand the many years of hard work, determination, disappointment, and adversity that are usually necessary to achieve success as an entrepreneur. All they see is the successful entrepreneur, who has worked to reach that position and who now drives a nice car and lives in a nice home. Because they do not understand the roots of successful entrepreneurship, they resent these people. They feel the money these successful fellow citizens have made should be taxed away and given to people and causes they feel are worthier.

Ronald Reagan wisely stated, "I think the best possible social program is a job." Entrepreneurs, through their hard work and determination, create more jobs and more opportunities, for more people, in more areas, using more different talents and abilities, than any other group in our society or in the world today.

Government and Capitalism

Unfortunately, enormous numbers of people in positions of political power the world over can look at successful corporations such as Amway and still fail to recognize their underlying capitalist principles. They don't realize that capitalism is not synonymous with greed. Greed means "me first." To be successful, capitalists must put their customers first.

Many critics of capitalism and free markets are elitists who, for political or ideological reasons, do not want ordinary people to make their own choices based on what they think is best for them. In this sense, capitalism also means *choice-ism*. Capitalism is based on freedom of choice, allowing you and encouraging you to spend your own money on whatever you feel is in your own best interests. America is a great country because it has the greatest freedom of choice in all areas of any country on earth. The greater the amount of economic freedom, the more dynamic the economy, the more jobs are created to serve that economy, and the wider the selection of goods and services at the lowest possible prices.

Whenever taxes are low and the size of government limited, more savings are accumulated and made available to invest in producing even more and better goods and services for the future. The smaller the government, the more money is available to capitalists, who see opportunities to put that money to work to achieve the highest possible returns by producing more products and services that people want, need, and will purchase. Smaller government leads to more innovation, more new jobs, and more opportunities for more people.

In 1980, in the United States, unemployment was at 11 percent, inflation was at 14 percent, and interest rates were at 21 percent. Economists and academics predicted the end of American prosperity and told us we had to look forward to a future of declining possibilities.

Then President Ronald Reagan successfully pushed legislation that slashed tax rates by 25 percent, unleashing a business expansion that continued, almost without interruption, until 2008. Between 1980 and 1990, capitalist America created seventeen million new jobs. The command economies of Central and Eastern Europe did not create a single new job, except for those in government.

From 1990 to 2000, capitalist America created twenty-two million new jobs and unleashed a technological revolution that created wealth at a speed and at a level never before seen in human history. Social democratic Europe created about three million new jobs, although it contained the same population. Most of those new jobs were in either government or export industries, producing products for sale to the United States.

Whenever governments are too large and taxes too high, the private sector is starved of the capital it needs to save, invest, and produce more goods and services. Government-created jobs are usually in areas that ordinary people, acting in their own best interests, do not want or need, or are unwilling to pay for. Bigger government and higher taxes lead to reduced opportunity, lower income for businesses and workers, the gradual decline of the economy, and the closing off of future opportunities.

In two thousand years of economic history, whenever government and taxes have been reduced, the private sector expanded and wealth was created. More people started new businesses, produced more products and services, and made them ever better so they could compete in dynamic markets.

One rule about money is that it invariably goes where it is welcome, stays where it is appreciated, and leaves where it is not. That is why, in order to attract investment, create jobs, and promote prosperity, cities, states, and entire nations need to make money welcome and appreciated. When they do not, it simply departs.

In March 2009, radio talk show host Rush Limbaugh announced that he was severing his remaining connections with New York. Limbaugh used to do his show from New York City before moving to Florida, a state with no income tax. He periodically returned to New York when he had meetings or there was a hurricane warning, and on those occasions the city and state taxed him for the income he earned for the days he worked. As New York continued to raise taxes on top earners, he'd had enough.

"I try to go [to New York] as little as possible. If it weren't for hurricanes down here, I would never go up there. New York is the escape valve in case hurricanes are showing up in our area, because of the loss of electricity," Limbaugh announced on his show.

> So I'll tell you what I'm going to do. I'm going to look for an alternative studio somewhere outside New York, perhaps Texas—another no-income-tax state—and I'm going to get . . . over there, when a hurricane starts coming our way. . . . I'll sell my apartment. I'll sell my condominium. I'm going to get out of there totally, 'cause this is just absurd, and it's ridiculous—and it isn't going to work. It's punishing the achievers for the mistakes and the lack of discipline on the part of a bunch of corrupt politicians that have run that city and state into the ground for I don't know how many years— and I, for one, am not going to take the blame for it.

Of course, Rush Limbaugh wasn't the only New Yorker to pack up his bags and go when taxes grew punitively high. A report by the Empire Center for New York State Policy found that from 2000 to 2008, 1.5 million New Yorkers left the high-tax state for greener, freer pastures. This was the largest population decline of any state during that period.[7]

Yet despite the huge exodus of human and financial capital

from New York, many of America's "best and brightest" intellectuals, academics, and liberal politicians believe that New York's example—ever-higher taxes, ever-more regulation, and ever-less liberty—should be the model for the rest of the country. And should you dare to disagree with them, that simply shows that you lack compassion, that you're indifferent to the suffering of the poor, or that you're a tool of special interests.

Ironically, while progressives in the United States willfully ignore the lessons of economic history, policy makers in nations once known for their embrace of socialism are adopting pro-growth policies. *Reason* magazine editor Michael C. Moynihan stated, "It is now unsurprising that Sweden has a significantly lower corporate tax rate than the United States, the Netherlands is a tax shelter utilized by millionaire rock bands like the Rolling Stones and U2, and a handful of countries in Central and Eastern Europe long ago realized Steve Forbes' dream of a flat income tax."[8]

That is why, now more than ever, Americans need to heed the wise words of Milton and Rose Friedman. "Whenever the free market has been permitted to operate," they wrote in their book *Free to Choose*, "wherever anything approaching freedom of opportunity has existed, the ordinary man has been able to attain levels of living never dreamed of before."[9]

The distinguished political theorist Kenneth Minogue has observed that "capitalism is what people do when you leave them alone."[10] America is great because it gives ordinary people the freedom to do extraordinary things, which is why capitalism is a fundamental component of the American Spirit.

CHAPTER 18

Education

We cannot be satisfied until every child in America—I mean every child—has the same chance for a good education that we want for our own children.

—Barack Obama, June 16, 2008

America is built on the philosophy of bootstrapping, or pulling yourself up by the use of your own talents and abilities. There is no tool better for doing just that than a good education. Poet Robert Frost once said that education means "hanging around until you've caught on." It's a bit more active than that, of course. "Learning is not attained by chance. It must be sought for with ardor and attended to with diligence," Abigail Adams wrote. Albert Einstein believed that "intellectual growth should commence at birth and cease only at death." Frost's thoughts may lead to great poetry, but Adams's and Einstein's philosophy will lead to success.

America offers more opportunities for more people to learn more subjects to improve their lives in more ways than any other country in the world. In America, you can learn anything you want or need to learn to achieve almost any goal you can set for yourself.

There are more than seventy-three thousand registered academic institutions of all kinds in America and more than thirty-six hundred colleges and universities. Such a competitive environment promotes educational excellence. American universities are the best in the world and attract students from more than one hundred fifty countries. The best and brightest graduates from American schools and universities are among the smartest and most accomplished people on the planet.

America is a great country because there are no limits to how much you can learn. And because your brain is like a muscle, the more you learn, the more you *can* learn. The more you use your mind, the better it performs, which is why more and more parents are homeschooling their children in order to increase their brainpower.[1]

Enrollment at for-profit universities that serve a wide range of student needs, from more traditional degrees to vocational and technical schools, has also increased significantly over the last two decades. Of course, these for-profits can be profitable only if they offer their students a valuable service.

Yet despite these positive trends, today American education stands at a crossroads. One path leads to increased government centralization, fewer parental choices, and a greater role for special interests. The other path leads to increased parental authority and a return to the constitutional principle that education policy is primarily a state and local affair and should not be set in Washington. Which path we ultimately go down will depend on the fate of school choice.

School Choice

Nothing has been more contentious in the field of education than the idea of school choice at the elementary and secondary levels. This is odd. Americans take it for granted that our stores will offer hundreds of brands of breakfast cereal and thousands of DVDs for rent. We expect to be able to choose from a wide variety of coffee drinks and a limitless supply of restaurants.

Yet we're expected to believe the school down the street is the best possible one for our children. Whether it offers foreign language classes, after-school activities, or excellent sports programs is irrelevant. It's the closest, and that's all we're supposed to need to know. Not only are Americans discouraged from shopping for public schools; they're usually not allowed to do so.

Of course, there are some very good public schools across the country; unfortunately, there are also some very, very bad ones. In many of the country's largest school districts, less than half of all children graduate. These failing schools are generally located in inner cities and serve poor minority students.

With their clientele trapped in a failing school system, those schools have virtually no incentive to improve because they face no penalties for failure. In Washington, DC's schools a few years ago, for example, most of the students were reading below grade level, yet virtually every teacher (98 percent) was rated above average.

The educational establishment's standard response to educational failure—the response by the teachers' unions and their liberal allies in Congress—is to call for massive spending increases in education. Yet today, while inflation-adjusted per-pupil spending has more than doubled since 1970—it now exceeds $10,000 per student per year—academic achievement has stagnated and high school graduation rates have remained flat.

In order to achieve meaningful educational reform, parents should be empowered to hold schools accountable through school choice. And the good news is that, in many cases, they are: today, millions of America's students exercise public school choice, attend private schools, and are schooled at home. Parents in Florida, for example, have access to details on school performance, including a grade from A to F for each school. Most important, they have a wide range of school choice options, including public school choice, online learning (such as the Florida Virtual School), and some private school choice.

Nevertheless, nearly three-quarters of America's children remain in government-assigned public schools—all too many of which fail even to provide a safe learning environment, let alone a good education. Scandalously, American teachers' unions are doing everything in their power to restrict parental choice in education, and thanks to their deep financial pockets, they often have the political clout to succeed. According to Heritage scholar Lindsey Burke:

> With a budget of more than $355 million, the National Education Association (NEA) spends more on campaign contributions than ExxonMobil, Microsoft, Wal-Mart, and

the AFL-CIO combined. During the 2007–2008 election cycle, the NEA and the American Federation of Teachers (AFT) spent more than $71 million on campaigns for issues and candidates, spending more than $100 per teacher in five states. In addition to the millions in campaign contributions, the NEA provides hundreds of thousands of dollars in member dues to left-leaning groups such as Planned Parenthood, the Service Employees International Union, and Health Care for America Now. The AFT funds groups that include the Rainbow PUSH coalition and ACORN.[2]

To understand the power of teachers' unions to block even the most promising educational reforms, consider the ongoing struggle over school choice in our nation's capital. Today, public schools in Washington, DC, enjoy the dubious distinction of leading the nation in violence while ranking among the lowest in academic performance. That's why the DC Opportunity Scholarship Program, launched in 2004, was such a breakthrough. According to a federally mandated evaluation, the use of an Opportunity Scholarship resulted in the equivalent of 3.7 months in additional learning for students. Moreover, these $7,500 scholarships, which enable students to attend a private school, are half the cost of the $15,000 per-pupil price tag for a year in a DC public school.

A president who pledged during his campaign to give "every child in America . . . the same chance for a good education that we want for our own children" might have been expected to strongly endorse the Opportunity Scholarship Program. Yet President Obama seems beholden to the teachers' unions, which vigorously oppose school choice. Although he attended (on a scholarship) the prestigious Punahou School in Hawaii, and he is sending his own children to one of the most prestigious schools in DC (Sidwell Friends), the president's fiscal year 2011 budget drastically cut funding for the Opportunity Scholarship Program.

Nor is President Obama unique in depriving other people's children of opportunities that his own children enjoy. Many members of Congress who support the administration's phasing out of funding for the Opportunity Scholarship Program exercised school choice for their own children. Indeed, 44 percent of senators in the 111th Congress sent their children to private schools—compared to an 11 percent rate for the general population. And the current secretary of education, Arne Duncan, chose to live outside Washington, DC, so that his children could attend Virginia's superior public school system.

Lindsey Burke summarized nicely the irony of the current situation:

Fifty years ago, African-Americans fought to enroll their children in public schools that would give their children an equal chance for a quality education. Boys and girls stood in the doorways of previously all-white schools that didn't want them, on the threshold of opportunity. But today's schools are not the same schools they fought to get into. Too many of today's schools are failing African-American and Hispanic students. In the 1950s, politicians stood in the door to keep African-American students out. Now, they are standing at the door to keep them in.[3]

Thankfully, however, the teachers' unions and their liberal allies are not all-powerful. On March 30, 2011, the US House of Representatives once again opened the doors to hope by voting to reauthorize and expand the DC Opportunity Scholarship Program. Predictably the White House opposed this legislation, wrongly claiming that the DC Opportunity Scholarship Program "has not yielded improved student achievement by its scholarship recipients compared to other students in D.C."[4] Nonetheless, in a last-minute compromise, funding for the DC Opportunity Scholarship Program was restored for 2011—a great victory for parents inside and outside Washington who have all too often seen their needs set aside in favor of the teachers' unions.

Unfortunately, even as the battle over the 2011 federal budget draws to a close, the battle over the 2012 federal budget moves to the forefront. Once again, labor leaders and their liberal allies will surely try to defund the DC Opportunity Scholarship Program. For the sake of America's children, they must not be allowed to succeed.

Tiffany's Testimony

Perhaps the last word on the debate over school choice in general, and the DC Opportunity Scholarship Program in particular, should go to Tiffany Dunston, a beneficiary of the program who testified before Congress in 2009:

> My family was overjoyed when I was selected to receive a DC Opportunity Scholarship (OSP) before entering my freshman year of high school. I had dreamt of going to Archbishop

Carroll high school but that was not possible. I lived with my grandmother who is disabled and she could not afford to send me to the school of my dreams. She applied for the scholarship because she wanted the best education for me.

Receiving a scholarship was a blessing for my family and put me on the path to success. I grew up in a neighborhood with a lot of poverty and crime. And there were such low expectations for kids in my neighborhood schools. I would watch kids hanging out on the streets and not going to school. My family also experienced our own tragedy. My motivation to get the best education possible was my cousin James who was shot and killed at 17. James was planning to attend college and play basketball. My cousin was going to be the first college graduate in my family, but he died before he was given that opportunity. Now I'm trying to step in his shoes and finish what he started. I am always thinking of what he could have done. To my family and to myself, I am a representation of what he could have done for my family and community. Through the DC OSP, I was afforded the opportunity to do just that. With the help of the scholarship my dream was realized. I had a say, a choice, in my education.

Now when I look back on my high school years I can definitely say that "I came a long way." This personal journey was made possible by my education at Archbishop Carroll. The environment at Carroll is so different from public schools in DC. From the activities and curriculum to the way we are expected to treat our peers and our studies, I was constantly pushed to be a better person and a better student. At a public school, there are constant distractions from school work. With the scholarship, I was able to attend a school that provided a caring environment as well as a school where one-on-one relationships with teachers were possible. Additionally, Archbishop Carroll gives you a moral education: what is right, and what not to do. The rigorous environment provided by Archbishop Carroll helped me to become the hardworking individual I am today.

I just finished my freshman year at Syracuse University, where I received almost a full scholarship. I'm excited to go back for my sophomore year, and plan on majoring in biochemistry and minoring in French. I do look at myself as a DC success story, but I am not the only one who has seen such achievement. I have friends who are in the same place as I am. They were able to have a scholarship and they're so happy with their experiences and how their future now looks.

I was lucky enough to receive the Opportunity Scholarship for all four years of high school. Had my scholarship been terminated halfway through, I would not have been able to graduate from Archbishop Carroll at the top of my class. I am so grateful for this opportunity—and sad that the other families won't have the same opportunity for their children if this program is taken away.

While I was able to come a long way, I see the challenges that kids in DC still face. I am determined to be a part of this fight to continue this scholarship for other students. I have been very blessed and would like others to have this same opportunity. I am determined to build a better life for myself and through this Opportunity Scholarship I am on that path. I want others in my community to have that chance as well.

You have the ability to give other D.C. children the opportunity I had. My education gave me the chance at a successful future. Please don't end a program that worked for me and is benefiting tons of other children. Three years from now I'll be walking across a stage receiving my college diploma. Without the OSP, none of this would have been possible.[5]

School choice programs in DC and elsewhere empower young Americans like Tiffany Dunston to realize their dreams. Isn't that what the American Spirit is all about?

CHAPTER 19

Money and Taxes

Every time in this century we've lowered the tax rates
across the board—on employment, on saving, investment
and risk-taking in this economy—revenues went up, not
down.

—Jack Kemp

Money

Your parents probably told you that money doesn't grow on
trees, and they were certainly correct. However, they probably
also explained that money *does* indeed grow.

Americans are famous for wanting to earn as much money as
possible. We work hard. We save. We invest. We try to achieve
financial independence, and we are known for supporting
charities.

Teaching the Value of Money

Consider Michael Holthouse. As an executive for Hewlett-Packard, he longed for entrepreneurial independence. So he left his successful career to start a new business. Six years later he sold his company, Paranet, to Sprint for $375 million. He had achieved a lifelong goal and decided to dedicate the rest of his life to helping at-risk kids. He wants every child to be able to rise above poverty. So Holthouse is trying to teach valuable life skills and the benefits of entrepreneurship.

In 2006 he and his wife created Lemonade Day, a program that on a set day every year encourages thousands of kids in cities across the United States to open a lemonade stand (with the help of an adult). The program provides workbooks for parents, teachers, and children in a backpack that the young entrepreneurs may keep. The materials demonstrate an age-appropriate plan for starting a drink stand. The kids are walked through the concepts of securing a loan, creating a product, marketing, managing the business, and deciding what to do with their profit.

And for the kids, that might be the best part. They get to keep their profits, which Holthouse says average around $200 per stand. The workbook places a great deal of emphasis on handling money responsibly. That means paying back loans, starting a savings account, and giving a portion of the profits to charity. In 2009 participants in the program gave some $500,000 to charities. For the participants, it's a chance to merge the qualities of an entrepreneur with the vivid imagination of a child as they decorate their stands and create unique marketing tools.

The fun and learning aren't limited to the kids. The adult workbook gives parents tools that some have parlayed into success in their own ventures. Holthouse said, "We have gotten call after call from parents saying, 'I was doing this with my child and these questions were really good. I started applying them to my landscape business and my sales have doubled.'"

He also noted how quickly the kids exhibit an understanding of money:

> There's always one kid who put the stand together. At the last minute, they invite one or two friends to help them run the stand. At the end of the day, the friends want to divide up the money equally. But the first kid—the entrepreneur—will say, "Wait a minute. I started this company. I put in the extra work." It is unreal to see them intuitively grasp these ideas about ownership and employment.[1]

Those concepts, of course, are protected in the adult world by American law that creates a framework within which wealth can be created, conserved, and passed on. Our society supports a free market economy (for the most part) that creates greater opportunities for financial independence than any other country on earth.

Upward Mobility

In 1860, Abraham Lincoln made the classic argument for upward mobility—what we today call the "American Dream":

I don't believe in a law to prevent a man from getting rich; it would do more harm than good. So while we do not propose any war upon capital, we do wish to allow the humblest man an equal chance to get rich with everybody else. . . . I want every man to have the chance—and I believe a black man is entitled to it—in which he *can* better his condition—when he may look forward and hope to be a hired laborer this year and the next, work for himself afterward, and finally to hire men to work for him! That is the true system.[2]

Lincoln's "true system" continues to generate opportunity and upward mobility today. Consider a report by Gerald Auten and Geoffrey Gee in the June 2009 *National Tax Journal.* "There was considerable income mobility of individuals in the U.S. economy over the 1996–2005 period," they found. "More than half of taxpayers (57.5 percent by one measure and 55 percent by another measure) moved to a different income quintile over this period. About half (56 percent by one measure and 42 percent by another) of those in the bottom income quintile in 1996 moved to a higher income group by 2005."

It's no wonder Americans tend to think of themselves as middle class. In a 2010 Pew survey, 50 percent of Americans called themselves middle class while a mere 8 percent considered themselves lower class. Those confident Americans are correct, since even if they're not exactly middle class this year, they have the opportunity to be and may well reach their goal in a year or two.

According to the old rhyme: "Money is a matter of functions four, a medium, a measure, a standard, a store." That is, money serves as a medium of exchange (a way of avoiding the inconveniences of bartering), a unit of account (a way of tracking profits and losses), a standard of deferred payment (a way of settling debts), and a store of value (a way of saving that inflation erodes).

Americans use money to help create, produce, and deliver products and services that people want, need, and will pay for. No other nation can boast of an Eli Whitney, a Robert Fulton, a Thomas Edison, and a Steve Jobs. Here, practical achievement is rewarded with financial gain.

Bill Gates became the richest man in America by creating Microsoft. But we've all benefited from his work. Microsoft created an operating system that made it simple to share information. This chapter is being drafted in Microsoft Word and will be shared over and over again by the authors and our editors before you read it. Imagine if we had to convert from one word processing program to another to edit each draft or retype each version completely by hand.

This standardization has also created untold thousands of jobs. If you're proficient in the Windows suite of programs, you can work in virtually any office without needing to spend days learning how the computer system works.

The Root of All Evil?

Critics of the free enterprise system like to cite what they claim is the biblical quotation: "Money is the root of all evil." But Paul the apostle actually wrote, "The love of money is the root of all evil."[3] It's not money, but avarice, that causes harm.

Nor is the Bible anti-profit. On the contrary, in the Old Testament, God blesses the patriarchs Abraham and Jacob by helping them become "very rich."[4] And in Matthew 25 and Luke 19, Jesus speaks of a master going away and entrusting his wealth to servants. The servants who reinvest the wealth are praised: "Well done, good and faithful servant. You have been faithful over a little; I will set you over much."[5] But the master condemns the "wicked and slothful servant"[6] who buried the money in the ground.

The provost of New York City's King's College, Dr. Marvin Olasky, explained in an anthology of writings by economic and social conservatives compiled by the Heritage Foundation:

> Christ's parables typically have multiple meanings, and these are no exceptions. Jesus was clearly referring to faithfulness, not just finance. But the parables also display the assumption that legitimate profit is praiseworthy. Over the past 2,000 years many Christians have criticized profit wrung from the poor, but some have gone on to attack profit-making enterprises generally—and that critique is thoroughly un-biblical. . . . The biblical goal is to make a profit and give much of it away.[7]

Americans generally support the idea of profit and reject the "something for nothing" mentality that destroys people and nations. That's why *socialism* is such a dirty word that even politicians who seem to favor it generally refuse to talk about it.

The Income Tax

It seems fair to most Americans that those who earn more should pay more taxes. But how much more is the subject of intense debate. Drawing on 2006 data (the most recent data available), Heritage scholar Curtis Dubay has demonstrated that a family in the top 20 percent of income earners earned 50 percent more than a family in the second 20 percent, yet paid 253 percent more in taxes. Even more strikingly a family's income in the top 20 percent income bracket was 122 percent higher than a family in the third 20 percent bracket, yet it paid a staggering 943 percent more in income taxes.[8]

Are these huge differences justified? Do they help make America a more just society, or is their real purpose to help politicians win votes by redistributing other people's incomes?

One way of making sure the rich pay more is through a proportional tax, also known as a flat tax. With a 10 percent flat tax, for example, someone earning $40,000 would pay $4,000 in taxes, and someone earning $80,000 would pay $8,000 in taxes.

Another way of collecting taxes is through a progressive tax. In such a system, someone earning $80,000 might pay $16,000 in taxes—a 20 percent tax rate—while someone earning less would pay taxes at a lower rate.

The United States has a progressive income tax. The great eighteenth-century social thinker Adam Smith, widely considered the father of modern economic thought, had some sympathy for this approach. "It is not unreasonable," he wrote in his seminal work, *The Wealth of Nations*, "that the rich should contribute to the public expense, not only in proportion to their revenue, but something more than in that proportion."[9] And indeed, in a society sharply divided between a handful of wealthy haves and a multitude of destitute have-nots, the moral case for a progressive income tax is compelling.

But the United States is not such a starkly unequal society. Judge Robert Bork stated,

> We are not talking about South American plutocrats living on million-acre estates that have been in their families for generations while peasants scrabble for a living on tiny plots of land. In America, "the rich" are overwhelmingly people—entrepreneurs, small businessmen, corporate executives, doctors, lawyers, etc.—who have gained their higher incomes through intelligence, imagination, and hard work.[10]

Depriving these Americans of their hard-earned financial rewards through higher tax rates does not seem particularly moral. Rather, it seems unjust.

The moral argument against progressive taxation is strongly reinforced by the economic argument. As tax rates grow increasingly progressive, incentives to work, save, and invest are reduced dramatically. As a result, fewer new businesses are launched, fewer new jobs are created, and both rich and poor are left worse off. A recent Heritage Foundation publication points out:

> Progressive taxation is problematic because it decreases the incentives for people to be productive and generate wealth

for themselves and the economy. For example, suppose a parent pays a child an hourly wage for helping around the house, but the wage decreases after each hour. The child's motivation will wither along with his hourly wages.

A progressive tax creates the same problem in the adult world. For the economy to grow, businesses must either produce increasing amounts of goods and services or create new ones. This in turn requires consistently higher investment in new production facilities and technologies and a motivated, productive workforce—therefore businesses and individuals must have financial resources to invest. Yet imposing higher tax rates on the last dollar earned shrinks the amount of money that a worker keeps as he creates more value. These taxes discourage all the wealth-creating activities mentioned above, since the last dollars earned are the ones most likely to be saved and invested rather than consumed.

Think of it this way: You spend your first dollars on necessities like food or rent, which everyone needs; but the more you earn, the more of your additional income you can save and invest—but also the more tax you pay. That's why lower tax rates on those dollars encourage working and saving, which, in turn, grow the economy.

History confirms common sense. High tax rates were reduced during the 1920s, the 1960s, and 1980s. In all three decades, lower tax rates contributed to increased investment, and robust economic growth followed. The economy grew by 59 percent from 1921 to 1929, 42 percent from 1961 to 1968, and 34 percent from 1982 to 1989.[11]

Even small changes in the tax code can have a major impact. For example, shortly after he became New York City's mayor, Rudy Giuliani cut the city's hotel tax from 6 percent to 5 percent. "This was a small step," he recalled,

> but important symbolically—no one could ever remember any tax ever being reduced in New York City. . . . I wanted to send a powerful message that I believed that lower taxes would stimulate more than enough business to offset any immediate loss in revenue. That's exactly what happened with the hotel tax. Within months, net revenue from the hotel tax was actually higher at five percent than it had been at six percent, since far more visitors were coming to the city.[12]

This is why Heritage's Curtis Dubay has called for a "flatter" tax code. "Under a flatter tax system," he wrote, "those who pay more income still pay more taxes, but that difference will be more proportional to income. . . . A code more in line with the flat tax is necessary to remove the barriers that block entrepreneurship and innovation."[13]

Americans usually oppose attacks on the financially successful people because they hope to be financially successful someday. And the statistics show they may well be! "Soak the rich" policies often just end up hurting the poor. Only people with money can invest and create jobs and opportunities. "Entrepreneurs must be allowed to retain the wealth they create because only they, collectively, can possibly know how to invest it productively among the millions of existing businesses and the innumerable visions of new enterprise in the world economy," George Gilder stated. Money flows to those who can use it best and create the most value from the way they deploy it.

The Regulatory Tax

While every American has heard about the income tax, not many are aware of the regulatory tax—the cost of all regulations (good, bad, and indifferent) imposed on Americans by the sixty or so government agencies (the Environmental Protection Agency, Securities and Exchange Commission, Food and Drug Administration, and so on) that contribute to the 157,000-page Code of Federal Regulations. Yet the regulatory tax is both hidden and huge. Heritage scholar James Gattuso reinforced this point:

> While the revenues and expenditures of the government are budgeted and accounted for each year, the costs of regulation are largely hidden from view, paid for indirectly via higher prices, fewer choices, and less innovation. The best estimates of the total cost, however, have come from a series of reports commissioned by the Small Business Administration (SBA). The latest such report was released [on September 22, 2010] by the SBA's Office of Advocacy, and the results are startling: Rules and regulations imposed from Washington now cost Americans $1.75 trillion each year. . . .
>
> No matter how you slice it, $1.75 trillion is a lot of money. It is far more than Americans pay in income taxes each year. It's about the same as the Gross Domestic Product of Italy. Per household, the regulatory tab works out to some

$15,000—almost as much as the average family spends on housing.[14]

Regulations often do more harm than good. For example, efficiency standards govern almost every appliance we buy, from battery chargers to water heaters. And they sound benign. But they're no friend to the consumer. "In many cases," wrote Heritage scholar Diane Katz, "the efficiency standards increase the price of appliances by more than consumers will recoup from energy savings."[15]

Fuel economy standards are no better. By increasing the cost of new cars, they cause more drivers to stick with older, less fuel-efficient vehicles. And research shows that by lowering the per-mile cost of driving, fuel standards actually induce people to drive more—defeating the purpose of having the standards in the first place.

As Gattuso noted, there is no magic bullet to lower the regulatory tax. Scholars at the Heritage Foundation and other institutions have come up with all sorts of creative ideas with which to fix or eliminate bad regulations. But to have these ideas implemented, Americans need to recognize that the hidden regulatory tax constitutes a major problem and to demand that their senators and representatives finally address it. Honesty, hard work, thrift, and transparency—not gimmicks and "gotcha" regulations—are the true hallmarks of the American Spirit.

CHAPTER 20

Courage

Courage is contagious. When a brave man takes a stand, the spines of others are often stiffened.

—Rev. Billy Graham

Courage

In "The Veteran," a short story published in 1896, Stephen Crane presented a memorable portrait of old Mr. Fleming, a courageous and revered Civil War veteran who seemed much like everyone else until the evening when his barn caught fire. Heedless of personal risk, Fleming ran into the blazing barn and saved most of his animals but at the cost of his own life: "When the roof fell in, a great funnel of smoke swarmed toward the sky, as if the old man's mighty spirit, released from its body—a little bottle—had swelled like the genie of fable. The smoke was tinted rose-hue from the flames, and perhaps the unutterable midnights of the universe will have no power to daunt the color of his soul."[1]

No one really understands how the bold colors of a hero's soul are formed, but we do know that without heroes, our nation would not endure. As Winston Churchill said, "Courage is rightly esteemed the first of human qualities, because it is the quality that guarantees all others."[2]

Americans are courageous in many ways. There were the firemen who ran into the burning towers on 9/11, lugging their gear up dozens of flights of steps in an attempt to do what they'd sworn to do—protect and serve. There are the police and the military, who run toward danger when others run away.

Few of us have that level of courage. Yet we demonstrate courage in different ways. We say what we think and stand up for our beliefs. We're willing to risk the criticism and the scorn of people who don't share our ideas. And when we're wrong, we admit it.

Moral Courage

Courage requires that you go forward, into the unknown, with no guarantee of success. You must move out of your comfort zone and stretch yourself by engaging in activities where you feel uncomfortable. Having courage means being willing to act boldly when the situation requires it.

Courage is built into the DNA of the American character. It took tremendous courage for millions of immigrants to leave home and family to come to America and start over in search of a better life. It required tremendous courage to move west, to face the open frontier, to risk lives and families in order to acquire a piece of the American Dream.

And it takes courage to stand up for what you know is right. For example, on October 18, 1986, President Ronald Reagan was meeting in Reykjavik, Iceland, with Soviet Premier Mikhail Gorbachev. The purpose was to broker an arms-control agreement that would end the deadly standoff of mutual assured destruction between the United States and the Soviet Union. At least, that *appeared* to be the purpose.

But after days of talks, just as the deal was about to be struck, Gorbachev looked across the table at Reagan, smiled, and said, "This all depends, of course, on you giving up SDI" (the Strategic Defense Initiative). Well, missile defense was one thing that Ronald Reagan would never give up. "I couldn't believe it," he later recalled. "I blew my top. . . . I realized that he had brought me to Iceland with one purpose, to kill the Strategic Defense Initiative." What Reagan did next stunned the world. He turned to Secretary of State George Shultz and said, "The meeting is over. Let's go, George, we're leaving." And he walked out. In her Reagan biography *When Character Was King*, Peggy Noonan went right to the heart of this story.

"Reagan had everything to gain—everything in the eyes of the world—if he had accepted the Reykjavik deal. He would have had the applause and respect of his foes, the thanks of a relieved world," Noonan wrote. "He would have been celebrated by history, known the pleasure of having given the world a gift of extraordinary and undreamed-of progress. Nothing but win all around him. But he wouldn't do it. . . . He didn't think it was right. And because he didn't do it, the Soviet Union finally fell." [3]

Now, leave Iceland and turn the calendar back thirty-one years to the evening of December 1, 1955, and we're in Montgomery, Alabama. City buses are carrying people home from work. On one bus all the seats are filled, including the section behind the rear doors, the only place blacks are allowed to sit.

Four white men board. The driver calls out to the four black passengers seated right behind the white section. "Get up," he tells them. "Let the white men have those seats." Three do as they're told. But the fourth doesn't budge. The other passengers turn and stare in stunned silence.

Rosa Parks is defying the unwritten, centuries-old code of racial subservience. She is also defying Alabama law. The driver gets off the bus and summons a policeman, who arrests the woman and takes her to jail.

Viewed from one perspective, Ronald Reagan and Rosa Parks couldn't have been more different. He was the most powerful person in the world, commander in chief of the armed forces of the United States. And she was one of the least powerful, an unknown black seamstress working in the back room of a department store in the Deep South before the passage of the Civil Rights Act. But in a more fundamental sense, they couldn't have been more admirably alike.

All the political power on earth couldn't have moved Reagan to do the wrong thing. And all the indignity and intimidation of racism couldn't keep Rosa Parks from doing the right thing. It was courage that made Ronald Reagan get up and leave. It was courage that kept Rosa Parks in her seat. And in those seemingly simple acts, each began building a bridge that would deliver millions of oppressed people to their God-given birthright of freedom and dignity. In Reagan's case, the people of Central and Eastern Europe; and in Parks's case, all citizens of the United States.

You demonstrate courage any time you set goals, especially when the probability of success is low. In fact, courage seems to be closely related to commitment. Courageous people make total commitments to their families, friends, and other people. They commit completely to their work, company, career, and business. Americans have courageous patience, the ability to work and wait for success, sometimes for many years, without giving up.

Selfless Courage

For an example of courageous dedication to his country and countrymen, look at Mike Monsoor. He hailed from a family that knew a thing or two about service. Mike's father was a marine, and his mother was a social worker. He grew up fighting asthma but persevered in high school to make the football team and become a superb athlete. In March 2001 Mike made the courageous decision that millions of men and women, his father included, have made: to serve our country. He enlisted in the navy.

Three years later he passed the rigorous training that less than one-third of his fellow trainees finish to become a Navy SEAL. He was now a frogman, one of the members of the navy's elite forces. In the spring of 2006 he was deployed to Ramadi, Iraq, where he served as a machine gunner and a communications operator in military operations against insurgents.

Through thirty-five heated firefights his SEAL team remained undeterred by the enemy. On September 29, 2006, Monsoor was providing security at a sniper lookout post with some other SEALs and eight Iraqi army soldiers. As Mike and his team scanned the area for the enemy, an insurgent threw a fragmentation grenade at the team's position. The grenade hit Monsoor in the chest before falling to the ground. In an instant every man on that roof could have died. But Mike Monsoor would not let that happen.

President George W. Bush described this SEAL's act of courage at Mike's Medal of Honor ceremony:

> Mike had a clear chance to escape, but he realized that the other two SEALs did not. In that terrible moment, he had two options—to save himself, or to save his friends. For Mike, this was no choice at all. He threw himself onto the grenade, and absorbed the blast with his body. One of the survivors puts it this way: "Mikey looked death in the face that day and said, you cannot take my brothers. I will go in their stead."

Monsoor died thirty minutes later from wounds sustained from the blast. He'd saved the lives of his two teammates and the Iraqi army soldiers on that roof. This courage was not lost on his SEAL brethren. Mike's funeral is believed to be the largest public gathering of SEALs in the history of the United States.

As the casket was taken from the hearse to the gravesite, SEALs lined the path and slapped their Tridents, a pin with the official symbol of having completed SEAL training, onto the top of Monsoor's coffin. President Bush said, "The procession went on nearly half an hour, and when it was all over, the simple wooden coffin had become a gold-plated memorial to a hero who will never be forgotten."[4]

Mike was a devoted Catholic, teammate, patriot, son, and defender of the American Spirit. He is survived by his mother, Sally; his father, George; his sister, Sara; and his two brothers, James and Joseph. He earned the gratitude of a nation.

The Courage of Our Convictions

Aristotle taught that courage was an essential virtue for excellence of character. He said courage was the golden mean between the qualities of rash behavior on the one side and cowardice on the other. Courage is a habit. You develop courage by acting courageously.

The Founding Fathers displayed tremendous courage. Even though most of them were rich and successful, they pledged their lives, their fortunes, and their sacred honor when they signed the Declaration of Independence, risking everything, including their lives. King George III would gladly have seen Washington, Franklin, Jefferson, Adams, and the rest executed for their courageous insurrection.

Americans have also shown courage by facing death in foreign wars to protect our way of life. Today Germany and Japan are true allies because of that courage.

Americans have demonstrated courage in nonphysical areas as well. They are willing to ask themselves the brutal questions and face the realities of their situations. They are not afraid to face the truth and deal with whatever life hands them.

Fear is easily the greatest enemy of mankind. And fear can be overcome only by confronting it and facing it down as many times as it takes until it disappears. Poet Ralph Waldo Emerson said, "Do the thing you fear and the death of fear is certain." Or as actor Glenn Ford said, "If you do not do the thing you fear, the fear controls your life."

Death and taxes are certainties in this life. But the only other thing that's guaranteed is that most things won't work out the way you expect them to. Winston Churchill learned from his experiences that "success is the ability to go from one failure to another with no loss of enthusiasm."[5]

We must find the courage to endure, to persevere, to keep on keeping on in the face of all failure, setbacks, and discouragement. America is great because it admires and rewards courage and perseverance at a higher level and more consistently than any other country.

Courage and perseverance are the twin qualities necessary to achieve greatly in all areas of life, and no one was more perseverant in the pursuit of his goals than Ronald Reagan. As his former attorney general Edwin Meese (who currently holds the Ronald Reagan Chair in Public Policy at the Heritage Foundation) told a Eureka College audience in 2008:

> A close cousin to courage is perseverance. [Reagan] used to say that if Congress only gave him half a loaf, he would take it and go back for more. This typified his relationship with the Soviet Union, as well. You may recall that the Soviets

established a set of intermediate range missiles across the border from our key Western European allies. NATO recommended that we set up a counterbalancing number of missiles pointing back at them but President Reagan strongly believed in a zero tolerance strategy.

Few agreed with his approach. Skeptics scoffed, and his own Secretary of State doubted the strategy would work. And initially, if predictably, the Soviets said "No." This led the president to install some missiles, yet he kept his "no missiles on the border" offer open to Soviet leadership. When conditions were right, and thanks to his perseverance, President Reagan and General Secretary Mikhail Gorbachev took down the missiles in the first-ever denuclearization effort in Europe.[6]

Perhaps the most important characteristic of political courage is the willingness to speak out clearly for what you believe in. That may mean going against the tide and refusing to compromise what you believe to be right for any reason or short-term gain. But so be it.

Ronald Reagan's entire political career was a testament to political courage. Former British prime minister Margaret Thatcher told a Heritage Foundation gathering in 1997:

Right from the beginning, Ronald Reagan set out to challenge everything that the liberal political elite of America accepted and sought to propagate. They believed that America was doomed to decline; he believed it was destined for further greatness. They imagined that sooner or later there would be convergence between the free Western system and the socialist Eastern system, and that some kind of social democratic outcome was inevitable; he, by contrast, considered that socialism was a patent failure which should be cast onto the trash-heap of history. They thought that the problem with America was the American people, though they did not quite put it like that; he thought that the problem with America was the American government, and he did put it just like that.[7]

America is a great country because in every crisis it finds ways to renew itself. Leaders emerge. Men and women of courage, character, and vision step up to carry the flag, make the hard decisions, and lead America forward. Among the hardest of those decisions will be summoning the political will to fix our broken entitlement system.

It won't be easy to fix Social Security, but if we don't, it will blow a multitrillion-dollar hole in our budget and bankrupt our grandchildren. It won't be easy to reduce the other entitlement programs—Medicare and Medicaid—but if we don't take these programs off autopilot, they'll grow until they swallow our entire federal budget.[8]

Americans will elect leaders with the courage to act, and we will eventually remove the drags on our enterprising spirit and repeal the encroachments on our fundamental freedoms. This is what the grassroots Tea Party movement is all about: Americans pushing back against Big Government. Hostile politicians and pundits like to claim Tea Partiers are racist, ignorant, or un-American. Nothing could be farther from the truth. They're true patriots who want to make this country's government once again the servant of "we the people," something many of our politicians have lost sight of in recent years.

It can be done. The Founders proved that when they wrote the most revolutionary political document of all time, the Declaration of Independence. Courage, both moral and physical, marks the true greatness of America. "The battle," said Patrick Henry, "is not to the strong alone; it is to the vigilant, the active, the brave."[9]

The American Spirit

"Through our great good fortune," said Supreme Court Justice Oliver Wendell Holmes Jr. in an 1884 Memorial Day address, "in our youth our hearts were touched with fire. It was given to us to understand at the outset that life is a profound and passionate thing."[10] Justice Holmes was referring to the generation that fought the Civil War. Subsequent generations of Americans, however, have also had their hearts touched with the fire of the American Spirit. Consequently, our life in this country continues to be "a profound and passionate thing."

In 1776, the American Spirit—exceptionally courageous, exceptionally optimistic, exceptionally enterprising, exceptionally devout, exceptionally generous, and exceptionally devoted to liberty—gave rise to a *novus ordo seclorum*, a "new order for the ages" in which ordinary men and women would at last be free to chart their own destinies. Over the years, this "new order" has been tried and tested many times and has emerged from every crisis stronger than ever because the mighty American Spirit that animates and inspires it is indomitable.

On December 25, 1982, in the course of his Christmas Day radio address to the nation, President Reagan read a letter from Ordnance Man, First Class, John Mooney, written to his parents aboard the aircraft carrier *Midway*. Mooney's letter is as fine a description of the American Spirit as anything we know:

Dear Mom and Dad, today we spotted a boat in the water, and we rendered assistance. We picked up sixty-five Vietnamese refugees. It was about a two-hour job getting everyone aboard, and then they had to get screened by intelligence and checked out by medical and fed and clothed and all that.

But now they're resting on the hangar deck, and the kids—most of them seem to be kids . . . are sitting in front of probably the first television set they've ever seen, watching *Star Wars*. Their boat was sinking as we came alongside. They'd been at sea five days and run out of water. All in all, a couple of more days and the kids would have been in pretty bad shape.

I guess every once in a while, we need a jolt like that for us to realize why we do what we do and how important, really, it can be. I mean, it took a lot of guts for those parents to make a choice like that to go to sea in a leaky boat in hope of finding someone to take them from the sea. So much risk! But apparently they felt it was worth it rather than live in a Communist country.

For all our problems, with the price of gas, and not being able to afford a new car or other creature comforts this year . . . I really don't see a lot of leaky boats heading out of San Diego looking for Russian ships out there. . . .

As they approached the ship, they were all waving and trying as best they could to say, "Hello, American sailor! Hello, freedom man!" It's hard to see a boat full of people like that and not get a lump somewhere between chin and belly button. And it really makes one proud and glad to be an American. People were waving and shouting and choking down lumps and trying not to let other brave men see their wet eyes. A lieutenant next to me said, "Yeah, I guess it's payday in more ways than one." (We got paid today.) And I guess no one could say it better than that.

It reminds us all of what America has been—a place a man or woman can come to for freedom. I know we're crowded and we have unemployment and we have a real burden with refugees, but I honestly hope and pray we can always find room. We have a unique society, made up of castoffs of all the world's wars and oppressions, and yet we're strong and free. We have one thing in common—no matter where our forefathers came from, we believe in freedom.

I hope we always have room for one more person, maybe an Afghan or a Pole or someone else looking for a place where he doesn't have to worry about his family's starving or a knock on the door in the night . . . and where all men who truly seek freedom and honor and respect and dignity for themselves and their posterity can find a place where they can . . . finally see their dreams come true and their kids educated and become the next generation of doctors and lawyers and builders and soldiers and sailors.

Love, John.[11]

The American Spirit is a force for good in a cruel and dangerous world. It is our firm conviction that it will rise up and soar once again, ready to meet today's challenges and those of the ages!

Further Reading

This book is based on the conviction that the birth of the United States of America brought something unique into being—a new way for people to relate to themselves, to their neighbors, and to the world at large. We call this unique "something" the American Spirit, and we believe that it is responsible for much of the economic, social, and political progress enjoyed by the world today. But this brief book is no more than an introduction to a vast and endlessly fascinating topic. To help you learn more about the American Spirit, we have put together a reading list made up of books that have instructed and inspired us. We hope your intellectual journey proves as exciting and illuminating as ours has been—and still is!

Chapter 1: Patriotism

Bennett, William. *The Spirit of America: Words of Advice from the Founders in Stories, Letters, Poems, and Speeches.* New York: Touchstone, 1997.

Berns, Walter. *Making Patriots.* Chicago: University of Chicago Press, 2002.

D'Souza, Dinesh. *What's So Great about America.* New York: Penguin, 2003.

———. "What's Great about America." Heritage Foundation First Principles Series Report #1. February 23, 2006.

Kirk, Russell. *Roots of American Order.* Wilmington, DE: Intercollegiate Studies Institute, 2003.

Kirkpatrick, Jeane J. "Defending U.S. Principles and Interests in the United Nations." In Edwin J. Feulner Jr., *The March of Freedom: Modern Classics in Conservative Thought.* Washington, DC: Heritage Books, 2003.

Noonan, Peggy. "Patriotism." In Edwin J. Feulner Jr., *Leadership for America: The Principles of Conservatism.* Dallas: Spence Publishing Company, 2000.

Pleszczynski, Wladyslaw. *Our Brave New World: Essays on the Impact of September 11.* Stanford, CA: Hoover Institution Press, 2002.

Podhoretz, Norman. *My Love Affair with America: The Cautionary Tale of a Cheerful Conservative.* New York: Encounter Books, 2001.

Spalding, Matthew. *The Founders' Almanac.* Washington, DC: Heritage Foundation, 2002.

Chapter 2: Freedom

Chafets, Zev. *Rush Limbaugh: An Army of One.* New York: Sentinel HC, 2010.

Goldwin, Robert A. *Why Blacks, Women and Jews Are Not Mentioned in the Constitution.* Washington, DC: AEI Press, 1990.

Heritage Foundation. *2011 Index of Economic Freedom.* Heritage Foundation and *Wall Street Journal,* 2011.

Meese, Edwin. "Freedom." In Edwin J. Feulner Jr., *Leadership for America: The Principles of Conservatism.* Dallas: Spence Publishing Company, 2000.

Sharlet, Robert. *The New Soviet Constitution of 1977: Analysis and Text.* Brunswick: OH: King's Court Communications, 1978.

Spalding, Matthew. *We Still Hold These Truths: Rediscovering Our Principles, Reclaiming Our Future.* Wilmington, DE: ISI Books, 2010.

Tracy, Brian. *The Way to Wealth.* Irvine, CA: Entrepreneur Press, 2006.

Chapter 3: Individuality

Adams, Nick. *America: The Greatest Good.* New York: iUniverse, 2010.

Hamilton, Alexander, James Madison, and John Jay. *The Federalist Papers.* New York: Tribeca Books, 2011.

Hickok, Eugene C. *Why States?: The Challenge of Federalism.* Washington, DC: Heritage Foundation, 2007.

Mill, John Stuart. *On Liberty.* Simon & Brown, 2011.

Sowell, Thomas. *A Conflict of Visions: Ideological Origins of Political Struggles.* New York: William Morrow, 1987.

Tracy, Brian. *Reinvention: How to Make the Rest of Your Life the Best of Your Life.* New York: AMACOM, 2009.

Chapter 4: Responsibility

Csorba, Les. *Trust: The One Thing That Makes or Breaks a Leader.* Nashville: Thomas Nelson, 2009.

Decter, Midge. *Liberal Parents, Radical Children.* New York: Coward, McCann & Geoghegan, 1975.

Feulner, Edwin J., Jr. *Intellectual Pilgrims: The Fiftieth Anniversary of the Mont Pelerin Society.* Washington, DC: Heritage Foundation, 1999.

Feulner, Edwin J., Jr., and Douglas Wilson. *Getting America Right.* New York: Crown Forum, 2006.

Gingrich, Newt. "Responsibility." In Edwin J. Feulner Jr., *Leadership for America: The Principles of Conservatism.* Dallas: Spence Publishing Company, 2000.

Goldwater, Barry. *The Conscience of a Conservative.* Bottom of the Hill Publishing, 2010.

Moore, Stephen. "Family." In *Indivisible: Social and Economic Foundations of American Liberty.* Washington, DC: Heritage Foundation, 2009.

Chapter 5: Optimism

Beach, William W., and Patrick D. Tyrrell. *The 2010 Index of Dependence on Government.* Washington, DC: Heritage Foundation, 2010.

Johnson, Paul. *A History of the American People.* New York: Harper Perennial, 1999.

Nisbet, Robert. *History of the Idea of Progress.* New Brunswick, NJ: Transaction Publishers, 1994.

Peale, Norman Vincent. *The Power of Positive Thinking.* New York: Fireside, 2003.

Rector, Robert. "How Poor Are America's Poor?: Examining the 'Plague' of Poverty in America." Heritage *Backgrounder,* August 27, 2007.

Revel, Jean-François. *How Democracies Perish.* Garden City, NY: Doubleday, 1984.

Tracy, Brian. *Create Your Own Future: How to Master the 12 Critical Factors of Unlimited Success.* Hoboken, NJ: Wiley, 2005.

Chapter 6: Foresight

Beach, William W., and Robert B. Bluey. *Will Growing Debt Undermine the American Dream?* Washington, DC: Heritage Foundation, 2010.

Coolidge, Calvin. "Speech on the Occasion of the 150th Anniversary of the Declaration of Independence." In Amy A. Kass, Leon R. Kass, and Diana Schaub, *What So Proudly We Hail: The American Soul in Story, Speech and Song.* Wilmington, DE: ISI Books, 2011.

Shattan, Joseph. *Architects of Victory: Six Heroes of the Cold War.* Washington, DC: Heritage Foundation, 1999.

Spalding, Matthew. *We Still Hold These Truths: Rediscovering Our Principles, Reclaiming Our Future.* Wilmington, DE: ISI Books, 2010.

Tracy, Brian. *Flight Plan: The Real Secret of Success.* San Francisco: Berrett-Koehler, 2009.

———. *How the Best Leaders Lead: Proven Secrets to Getting the Most Out of Yourself and Others.* New York: AMACOM, 2010.

Chapter 7: Good Citizenship

Berger, Peter, John Richard Neuhaus, and Michael Novak. *To Empower People: From State to Civil Society.* Washington, DC: AEI Press, 1995.

Bork, Robert H. *Slouching Towards Gomorrah: Modern Liberalism and American Decline.* New York: Regan Books, 1996.

Forbes, Steve, and John Prevas. *Power Ambition Glory.* New York: Crown Business, 1999.

Kolakowski, Leszek. *Freedom, Fame, Lying, and Betrayal.* Boulder, CO: Westview Press, 1999.

Nisbet, Robert. *The Quest for Community: A Study in the Ethics of Order and Freedom.* Wilmington, DE: Intercollegiate Studies Institute, 2010.

Powell, Jim. *The Triumph of Liberty.* New York: Free Press, 2000.

Rasmussen, Scott, and Douglas Schoen. *Mad as Hell: How the Tea Party Movement Is Fundamentally Remaking the Two-Party System.* New York: HarperCollins, 2010.

Chapter 8: Honesty

Bennett, William J. "Truth." In Edwin J. Feulner Jr., *Leadership for America: The Principles of Conservatism.* Dallas: Spence Publishing Company, 2000.

Chambers, Whittaker. "A Letter to My Children." In Edwin J. Feulner Jr., *The March of Freedom: Modern Classics in Conservative Thought.* Washington, DC: Heritage Foundation, 2002.

———. *Witness.* Washington, DC: Regnery, 1987.

Covey, Stephen. *The 7 Habits of Highly Effective People.* New York: Free Press, 2004.

Flexner, James Thomas. *Washington: The Indispensable Man.* Back Bay Books, 1994.

Kidder, Rushworth. *How Good People Make Tough Choices.* New York: Harper Paperbacks, 2009.

Lewis, C. S. *The Abolition of Man.* Lits, 2010. HarperOne, 2001.

Thomas, Clarence. *My Grandfather's Son: A Memoir.* New York: Harper, 2007.

———. "Character." In Edwin J. Feulner Jr., *Leadership for America: The Principles of Conservatism.* Dallas: Spence Publishing Company, 2000.

Chapter 9: Something for Nothing

Bartley, Robert. *The Seven Fat Years: And How to Do It Again.* New York: Free Press, 1995.

Bradley, Kiki, and Robert Rector. "Confronting the Unsustainable Growth of Welfare Entitlements: Principles of Reform and the Next Steps." Heritage *Backgrounder* no. 2427, June 24, 2010.

DeVos, Rich. *Compassionate Capitalism.* New York: Plume, 1994.

Friedman, Milton, and Rose Friedman. *Free to Choose: A Personal Statement.* New York: Mariner Books, 1990.

Hayek, F. A. "Responsibility and Freedom." In Edwin J. Feulner Jr., *The March of Freedom: Modern Classics in Conservative Thought.* Washington, DC: Heritage Foundation, 2002.

Heinlein, Robert. *The Moon Is a Harsh Mistress.* New York: Orb Books, 1997.

Kristol, Irving. *The Neoconservative Persuasion: Selected Essays 1942–2009.* New York: Basic Books, 2011.

MacDonald, Heather. *The Burden of Bad Ideas.* Chicago: Ivan R. Dee, 2001.

Chapter 10: Faith

Cromartie, Michael. *Religion and Politics in America: A Conversation.* Lanham, MD: Rowman and Littlefield, 1995.

Evans, M. Stanton. *The Theme Is Freedom: Religion, Politics and the American Tradition.* Washington, DC: Regnery, 1996.

Federer, William J. *Three Secular Reasons Why America Should Be Under God.* St. Louis, MO: Amerisearch, 2004.

Gregg, Gary. *Vital Remnants: America's Founding and the Western Tradition.* Wilmington, DE: ISI Books, 2006.

Kristol, Irving. *The Neoconservative Persuasion: Selected Essays 1942–2009.* New York: Basic Books, 2011.

Lewis, C.S. *Mere Christianity.* San Francisco: HarperSanFrancisco, 2001.

Marshall, Jennifer. *Understanding America: Why Does Religious Freedom Matter?* Washington, DC: Heritage Foundation, 2011.

Neuhaus, Richard John. *The Naked Public Square.* Grand Rapids: Eerdmans, 1996.

Podhoretz, Norman. *The Prophets: Who They Were, What They Are.* New York: Free Press, 2010.

Spalding, Matthew. *The Founders' Almanac.* Washington, DC: Heritage Foundation, 2002.

———. *We Still Hold These Truths: Rediscovering Our Principles, Reclaiming Our Future.* Wilmington, DE: ISI Books, 2010.

Chapter 11: The Law

Biskupic, Joan. *American Original: The Life and Constitution of Supreme Court Justice Antonin Scalia.* New York: Farrar, Straus & Giroux, 2009.

Bork, Robert. *The Tempting of America.* New York: Free Press, 1997.

Kafka, Franz. *The Trial.* Charleston, SC: CreateSpace, 2010.

Moffit, Robert. "How to Roll Back the Administrative State." Heritage Foundation, Center for Policy Innovation Discussion Paper no. 1.

Rosenzweig, Paul, and Brian W. Walsh. *One Nation Under Arrest: How Crazy Laws, Rogue Prosecutors, and Activist Judges Threaten Your Liberty.* Washington, DC: Heritage Foundation, 2010.

Spalding, Matthew. *We Still Hold These Truths: Rediscovering Our Principles, Reclaiming Our Future.* Wilmington, DE: ISI Books, 2010.

Chapter 12: Tolerance and Open-Mindedness

Bloom, Allan. *The Closing of the American Mind*. New York: Simon & Schuster, 1988.

Bork, Robert H. *Slouching Towards Gomorrah: Modern Liberalism and American Decline*. New York: Regan Books, 1996.

Buckley, William F. *Miles Gone By: A Literary Autobiography*. Washington, DC: Regnery, 2005.

Feulner, Edwin J., Jr. *Intellectual Pilgrims: The Fiftieth Anniversary of the Mont Pelerin Society*. Washington, DC: Heritage Foundation, 1999.

Hook, Sidney. *Out of Step: An Unquiet Life in the 20th Century*. New York: Carroll & Graff, 1988.

Kolakowski, Leszek. *Freedom, Fame, Lying, and Betrayal*. Boulder, CO: Westview Press, 1999.

Kristol, Irving. *The Neoconservative Persuasion: Selected Essays 1942–2009*. New York: Basic Books, 2011.

Spalding, Matthew. *We Still Hold These Truths: Rediscovering Our Principles, Reclaiming Our Future*. Wilmington, DE: ISI Books, 2010.

Chapter 13: Idealistic Realism

Burnham, James. *The Machiavellians: Defenders of Freedom*. Washington, DC: Gateway Editions, 1987.

Kissinger, Henry. *Diplomacy*. New York: Simon & Schuster, 1995.

Kolakowski, Leszek. *Freedom, Fame, Lying, and Betrayal*. Boulder, CO: Westview Press, 1999.

Meese, Edwin. *The Heritage Guide to the Constitution*. Washington, DC: Heritage Foundation, 2005.

Peacock, Anthony A. *How to Read the Federalist Papers*. Washington, DC: Heritage Foundation, 2010.

Reagan, Ronald. *An American Life: The Autobiography*. New York: Simon & Schuster, 1990.

Richards, Jay. *What Causes Poverty in America?* Washington, DC: Heritage Foundation, 2010.

Chapter 14: Pragmatism

Bawer, Bruce. "The Closing of the Liberal Mind." In Adam Bellow, *New Threats to Freedom*. West Conshohocken, PA: Templeton Press, 2010.

Crocker, H. W. *Don't Tread on Me*. New York: Crown Forum, 2006.

Edwards, Lee. *The Conservative Revolution: The Movement That Remade America*. New York: Free Press, 1999.

———. *A Brief History of the Modern Conservative Movement*. Washington, DC: Heritage Foundation, 2004.

———. *William F. Buckley Jr.: The Maker of a Movement*. Wilmington, DE: ISI Books, 2010.

Friedman, Milton. "Capitalism and Freedom." In Edwin J. Feulner Jr., *The March of Freedom: Modern Classics in Conservative Thought*. Washington, DC: Heritage Foundation, 2002.

McCullough, David. *1776*. New York: Simon & Schuster, 2006.
Schweikart, Larry, and Michael Allen. *A Patriot's History of the United States*. New York: Penguin, 2004.

Chapter 15: Problem Solving

De Tocqueville, Alexis. *Democracy in America*. New York: Library of America, 2004.
Goldberg, Jonah. *Liberal Fascism: The Secret History of the American Left from Mussolini to the Politics of Meaning*. New York: Doubleday, 2008.
Goldwin, Robert. *From Parchment to Power: How James Madison Used the Bill of Rights to Save the Constitution*. Washington, DC: AEI Press, 1998.
Kristol, Irving. *The Neoconservative Persuasion: Selected Essays 1942–2009*. New York: Basic Books, 2011.
Murray, Charles. *The Happiness of People*. Washington, DC: AEI Press, 2009.
Spalding, Matthew. *We Still Hold These Truths: Rediscovering Our Principles, Reclaiming Our Future*. Wilmington, DE: ISI Books, 2010.
Wilson, James Q. *Thinking about Crime*. New York: Vintage, 1985.

Chapter 16: Generosity

Behrman, Greg. *The Most Noble Adventure: The Marshall Plan and How America Helped Rebuild Europe*. New York: Free Press, 2008.
Brooks, Arthur. *Who Really Cares: The Surprising Truth about Compassionate Conservatism*. New York: Basic Books, 2007.
Crutchfield, Leslie, and Heather Grant. *Forces for Good: The Six Practices of High-Impact Nonprofits*. San Francisco: Jossey-Bass, 2007.
DeVos, Rich. *Compassionate Capitalism*. New York: Plume, 1994.
Gaudiani, Claire. *Generosity Unbound: How American Philanthropy Can Strengthen the Economy and Expand the Middle Class*. Broadway Publications, 2010.
Malloch, Theodore Roosevelt. *Being Generous*. West Conshohocken, PA: Templeton Press, 2009.
Miller, John J. *A Gift of Freedom: How the John M. Olin Foundation Changed America*. New York: Encounter Books, 2005.
Olasky, Marvin. *The Tragedy of American Compassion*. Wheaton, IL: Crossway Books, 2008.

Chapter 17: Capitalism

Becker, Gary. "Competition." In Edwin J. Feulner Jr., *The March of Freedom: Modern Classics in Conservative Thought*. Washington, DC: Heritage Foundation, 2002.
Butler, Eamonn. *The Best Book on the Market: How to Stop Worrying and Love the Free Economy*. Chichester, UK: Capstone, 2008.
DeVos, Rich. *Compassionate Capitalism*. New York: Plume, 1994.
Forbes, Steve. *How Capitalism Will Save Us*. New York: Crown Business, 2011.

Friedman, Milton. *Capitalism and Freedom*. Chicago: University of Chicago Press, 1962.

Friedman, Milton, and Rose Friedman. *Free to Choose: A Personal Statement*. New York: Mariner Books, 1990.

Gilder, George. *Wealth and Poverty*. New York: Basic Books, 1981.

———. *The Spirit of Enterprise*. New York: Touchstone Books, 1985.

———. *The Israel Test*. Minneapolis: Richard Vigilante Books, 1985.

Holmes, Kim R., and Matthew Spalding. *Understanding America: Why Does Economic Freedom Matter?* Washington, DC: Heritage Foundation, 2011.

Lambro, Donald. *Land of Opportunity: The Entrepreneurial Spirit in America*. Boston: Little, Brown, 1986.

Malloch, Theodore Roosevelt. *Spiritual Enterprise: Doing Virtuous Business*. New York: Encounter Books, 2009.

Mariotti, Steve. *Entrepreneurship*. Upper Saddle River, NJ: Prentice Hall, 2007.

Miller, John J. *A Gift of Freedom: How the John M. Olin Foundation Changed America*. New York: Encounter Books, 2005.

Moynihan, Michael C. "The Anticapitalists." In Adam Bellow, *New Threats to Freedom*. West Conshohocken, PA: Templeton Press, 2010.

Novak, Michael. *The Spirit of Democratic Capitalism*. Lanham, MD: Madison Books, 1990.

Schramm, Carl. *The Entrepreneurial Imperative*. New York: HarperBusiness, 2006.

Tracy, Brian, *Victory!* New York: AMACOM, 2002.

Van Andel, Jay. *An Enterprising Life*. London: Collins, 1998.

Chapter 18: Education

Bast, Joseph L., and Herbert J. Walberg. *School Choice: The Findings*. Washington, DC: Cato Institute, 2007.

Bortins, Leigh. *The Core: Teaching Your Child the Foundations of a Classical Education*. New York: Palgrave Macmillan, 2010.

Edwards, Lee. *Reading the Right Books*. Washington, DC: Heritage Foundation, 2009.

Enlow, Robert, and Lenore Ealy. *Milton Friedman's Voucher Idea at Fifty*. Washington, DC: Cato Institute, 2007.

Ferguson, Andrew. *Crazy U: One Dad's Crash Course in Getting His Kid into College*. New York: Simon & Schuster, 2011.

Friedman, Milton, and Rose Friedman. *Free to Choose: A Personal Statement*. New York: Mariner Books, 1990.

Zmirak, John. *Choosing the Right College 2010–2011*. Wilmington, DE: Intercollegiate Studies Institute, 2009.

Chapter 19: Money and Taxes

Bork, Robert H. *Slouching Towards Gomorrah: Modern Liberalism and American Decline*. New York: Regan Books, 1996.

Carbone, Leslie, and Jay Richards. *What Makes the Economy Grow?* Washington, DC: Heritage Foundation, 2010.

Hazlitt, Henry. *Economics in One Lesson.* New York: Three Rivers Press, 1988.

Kemp, Jack. *The American Idea: Ending Limits to Growth.* Washington, DC: American Studies Center, 1984.

Laffer, Arthur. *The End of Prosperity: How Higher Taxes Will Doom the Economy—If We Let It Happen.* New York: Threshold Editions, 2009.

Laffer, Arthur, and Stephen Moore. *Return to Prosperity: How America Can Regain Its Superpower Status.* New York: Threshold Editions, 2010.

Moore, Gary. *Ten Golden Rules for Financial Success.* Grand Rapids: Zondervan, 1997.

Olasky, Marvin. "Profit: Prophets and Profit." In *Indivisible: Social and Economic Foundations of American Liberty.* Washington, DC: Heritage Foundation, 2010.

Sennholz, Hans. *Taxation and Confiscation.* Irvington-on-Hudson, NY: Foundation for Economic Education, 1993.

Shlaes, Amity. *The Forgotten Man: A New History of the Great Depression.* New York: Harper Perennial, 2008.

Chapter 20: Courage

Churchill, Winston. *Never Give In: The Best of Winston Churchill's Speeches.* New York: Hyperion, 2003.

Crane, Stephen. "The Veteran." In Amy A. Kass, Leon R. Kass, and Diana Schaub, *What So Proudly We Hail: The American Soul in Story, Speech and Song.* Wilmington, DE: ISI Books, 2011.

Manchester, William. *American Caesar: Douglas MacArthur 1880–1964.* Boston: Little, Brown, 1978.

Noonan, Peggy. *When Character Was King: A Story of Ronald Reagan.* New York: Penguin, 2002.

Reagan, Ronald. *An American Life: The Autobiography.* New York: Simon & Schuster, 1990.

———. *Speaking My Mind: Selected Speeches.* New York: Simon & Schuster, 1989.

Talbott, Frederick. *Winston Churchill on Courage: Timeless Wisdom for Persevering.* Nashville: Thomas Nelson, 2006.

Thatcher, Margaret. "Courage." In Edwin J. Feulner Jr., *Leadership for America: The Principles of Conservatism.* Dallas: Spence Publishing Company, 2000.

Notes

Introduction

1. Midge Decter, "Long Live the Revolution," Heritage Foundation, April 21, 1995, www.heritage.org/research/lecture/long-live-the-revolution.

Chapter 1: Patriotism

1. Thomas Jefferson, letter to Thomas Jefferson Smith, cited in Matthew Spalding, *The Founders' Almanac* (Washington, DC: Heritage Foundation, 2002), 177.
2. Peggy Noonan, "Patriotism," in Edwin J. Feulner Jr., *Leadership for America: The Principles of Conservatism* (Dallas: Spence Publishing Company, 2000), 167–68.
3. Father Edward J. Burns, "The Priests of September 11, 2001: Men of Word and Sacrament," http://www.vocation.com/DiscernmentLibraryItem.aspx?id=440.
4. Media Research Center, "Only Gore's Take Relevant; McCain as CBS's Expert; Hsia's Light Penalty; Powell Hit by MTV with

Anti-U.S. Views; Lay Worse," *Cyber Alert*, February 15, 2002, http://www.mediaresearch.org/cyberalerts/2002/cyb20020215.asp.

5. David Azerrad, "Taking Exception to American Exceptionalism," *Foundry*, Heritage Foundation, December 22, 2010.

6. Jeane Kirkpatrick, cited in Edwin J. Feulner Jr., *The March of Freedom: Modern Classics in Conservative Thought* (Washington, DC: Heritage Books, 2003), 474–75.

7. Joseph Story, *Commentaries on the Constitution* (1833).

8. Dinesh D'Souza, "What's Great About America," Heritage Foundation First Principles Series Report no. 1, February 23, 2006.

9. Cited in ibid.

Chapter 2: Freedom

1. John Adams, "A Dissertation on the Canon and the Feudal Law" (*Boston Gazette*, August 12–October 21, 1765).

2. Robert Sharlet, *The New Soviet Constitution of 1977: Analysis and Text* (Brunswick, OH: King's Court Communications, 1978), 89.

3. Robert Moffit, "Rx for a Republic: Recovering Liberty in Health Care," *Insider*, Fall/Winter 2010, 18.

4. Address by Patrick Henry at the Second Virginia Convention, St. John's Church, Richmond, Virginia, March 20, 1775.

5. Azadeh Moaveni, "Stars (and Stripes) in Their Eyes," *Washington Post*, June 1, 2008.

6. Edwin Meese, "Freedom," in Edwin J. Feulner Jr., *Leadership for America: The Principles of Conservatism* (Dallas: Spence Publishing Company, 2000), 223–24.

7. Terry Miller, "The U.S. Loses Ground on Economic Freedom," *The Wall Street Journal*, January 12, 2011.

8. Meese, "Freedom," 230.

Chapter 3: Individuality

1. *Papers of Dr. James McHenry on the Federal Convention of 1787*, Entry for September 18. Found in *The American Historical Review*, Vol. 11, No. 3. (April 1906), 618.

2. Nick A. Adams, *America: The Greatest Good* (New York: iUniverse, 2010), 35, 40.

3. James Fenimore Cooper, "On Individuality," *The American Democrat* (Cooperstown: H. & E. Phinney, 1838), 182.
4. Thomas Jefferson, "Answers by Mr. Jefferson, to questions addressed to him by Monsieur de Meusnieg. 270., nd C: , to Questions 38)ume XIl Convention. See entry r, author of that part of the Encyclopedie Methodique, entitled Economic Politique et Diplomatique," *The Writings of Thomas Jefferson*, Vol. IX, (Washington DC: Taylor & Maury, 1854), 270.
5. Thomas Sowell, *A Conflict of Visions: Ideological Origins of Political Struggles* (New York: William Morrow, 1987), 20.
6. Stephen Jay Gould, *The Panda's Thumb* (New York: W.W. Norton & Co, 1980), ch. 13.
7. Mike Franc, "Time to Set Aside Set-Asides?" *National Review Online*, January 27, 2009.
8. Eugene C. Hickok, *Why States?: The Challenge of Federalism* (Washington, DC: Heritage Foundation, 2007), 80.

Chapter 4: Responsibility

1. George Washington, Circular to the States, June 14, 1783, *George Washington: A Collection*, ed. W.B. Allen (Indianapolis: Liberty Classics, 1988), 241.
2. Stephen Moore, "Family," in *Indivisible: Social and Economic Foundations of Economic Liberty* (Washington, DC: Heritage Foundation), 43–44.
3. Ryan Messmore, "Taking Time for Justice," Heritage *Commentary*, December 1, 2008.
4. Cited in Edwin J. Feulner Jr. and Douglas Wilson, *Getting America Right* (New York: Crown Forum, 2006), 56–58.
5. F. A. Hayek, *The Road to Serfdom* (Chicago: University of Chicago Press, 1994). Quoted in "Seven Principles of a Free Society," Presidential Address by Edwin J. Feulner Jr. to the 1997 Regional Meeting of the Mont Pelerin Society, in *Intellectual Pilgrims: The Fiftieth Anniversary of the Mont Pelerin Society* (Washington, DC: Heritage Foundation, 1999), 38.
6. Sean Sposito, "One man's imperative to give," *Boston Globe*, July 18, 2009.
7. Newt Gingrich, "Responsibility," in Edwin J. Feulner Jr., *Leadership for America: The Principles of Conservatism* (Dallas: Spence Publishing Company, 2000), 84.

Chapter 5: Optimism

1. NBC poll from AEI data, 34.
2. Douglas Holtz-Eakin, Harvey Rosen, and Robert Weathers, "Horatio Alger Meets the Mobility Tables," *Small Business Economics* 14, no. 4 (2000): 243–74.
3. Interview with John Mackey, www.endervidualism.com/salon/intvw/mackey.htm.
4. Milton Friedman, "Poverty and Equality," YouTube, http://www.youtube.com/watch?feature=player_embedded&v=fKc6esIi0_U.
5. http://www.census.gov/hhes/www/cpstables/032009/rdcall/2_001.htm.
6. Robert Rector, "How Poor Are America's Poor? Examining the 'Plague' of Poverty in America," Heritage *Backgrounder*, August 27, 2007.
7. "Milton Friedman Interviewed," *The Times Herald*, December 1, 1978.
8. Revel's pessimism resembled that of the great conservative thinker Whittaker Chambers, who believed, when he abandoned communism, that he was leaving "the winning side for the losing side."
9. Although this quotation is widely attributed to Alexander Tytler, its origins remain unknown for certain.
10. William W. Beach and Patrick D. Tyrrell, *The 2010 Index of Dependence on Government* (Washington, DC: Heritage Foundation, 2010), 27.
11. Chris Christie, "We Are Teetering on the Edge of Disaster," quoted on realclearpolitics.com, February 16, 2011.

Chapter 6: Foresight

1. Cited in Matthew Spalding, *We Still Hold These Truths: Rediscovering Our Principles, Reclaiming Our Future* (Wilmington, DE: ISI Books, 2010), 220.
2. Ibid., 221.
3. Joseph Shattan, *Architects of Victory: Six Heroes of the Cold War* (Washington, DC: Heritage Foundation, 1999), 246.
4. Ibid., 293.
5. William W. Beach and Robert B. Bluey, *Will Growing Government Debt Undermine the American Dream?* (Washington, DC: Heritage Foundation, 2010), 1.

6. All recommendations are adopted from *Solutions for America*, (Washington, DC: Heritage Foundation, 2010), 7–8.
7. Chuck Donovan, "The Car-Wreck Generation," *USA Today*, November 18, 2010.

Chapter 7: Good Citizenship

1. Alexis de Tocqueville, *Democracy in America*, cited in Jim Powell, *The Triumph of Liberty* (New York: Free Press, 2000), 342.
2. Robert H. Bork, *Slouching Towards Gomorrah: Modern Liberalism and American Decline* (New York: Regan Books, 1996), 11.
3. Scott Rasmussen and Douglas Schoen, *Mad as Hell: How the Tea Party Movement Is Fundamentally Remaking the Two-Party System* (New York: HarperCollins, 2010), 26.
4. Ibid., 55.
5. Matthew Spalding, "Reclaiming America: Why We Honor the Tea Party Movement," Heritage *WebMemo* no. 2961, July 15, 2010, 3.
6. Leszek Kolakowski, *Freedom, Fame, Lying, and Betrayal* (Boulder, CO: Westview Press, 1999), 7–8.
7. Steve Forbes and John Prevas, *Power Ambition Glory* (New York: Crown Business, 2009), 64.

Chapter 8: Honesty

1. Clarence Thomas, "Character," in Edwin J. Feulner Jr., *Leadership for America: The Principles of Conservatism* (Dallas: Spence Publishing Company, 2000), 26–27.
2. Clarence Thomas, *My Grandfather's Son: A Memoir,* (New York: Harper 2007), pg. 101.
3. Robert Moffit, "Repair? No, Repeal ObamaCare," Heritage *Commentary*, August 13, 2010.
4. Whittaker Chambers, "A Letter to My Children," cited in Edwin J. Feulner Jr., *The March of Freedom: Modern Classics in Conservative Thought* (Washington, DC: Heritage Books, 2003), 297–98.
5. Thomas Paine, "Age of Reason," *Collected Writings: Common Sense, the Crisis, and Other Pamphlets, Articles, and Letters ; Rights of Man ; The Age of Reason*, ed. Eric Foner, (New York: Literary Classics of the United States, 1995), 666. (Paine's work originally published 1794.)

6. Compare the current climate of moral relativism with the views of the great nineteenth-century British historian Lord Acton: "History does teach that right and wrong are real distinctions. Opinions alter, manners change, creeds rise and fall, but the moral law is written on the tablets of eternity." Cited in Jim Powell, *The Triumph of Liberty* (New York: Free Press, 2000), 350.

7. William J. Bennett, "Truth," in Feulner, *Leadership for America*, 154.

8. C. S. Lewis, *The Abolition of Man*, posted by the Augustine Club at Columbia University, augustine@columbia.edu.

Chapter 9: Something for Nothing

1. Cited in Matthew Spalding, *The Founders' Almanac* (Washington, DC: Heritage Foundation, 2002), 53.

2. Irving Kristol, *The Neoconservative Persuasion: Selected Essays, 1942–2009* (New York: Basic Books, 2011), 99–101.

3. Ibid., 261–62.

4. Kiki Bradley and Robert Rector, "Confronting the Unsustainable Growth of Welfare Entitlements: Principles of Reform and the Next Steps," Heritage *Backgrounder* no. 2427.

5. William F. Buckley Jr., cited in Lee Edwards, *William F. Buckley Jr.: The Maker of a Movement* (Wilmington, DE: ISI Books, 2010), 131.

6. Stuart Butler, Alison Acosta Fraser, and James Gattuso, "What Should Be Done About the Financial Markets?" Heritage *WebMemo* no. 2010, September 19, 2008.

7. Stuart Butler, "Time to End the TARP Bailout Program," Heritage *WebMemo* no. 2174, December 15, 2008.

8. *Solutions for America* (Washington, DC: Heritage Foundation, 2010), 4.

9. F. A. Hayek, "Responsibility and Freedom," cited in Edwin J. Feulner Jr., *The March of Freedom: Modern Classics in Conservative Thought* (Washington, DC: Heritage Books, 2003), 65.

Chapter 10: Faith

1. Jennifer Marshall, *Understanding America: Why Does Religious Freedom Matter?* (Washington, DC: Heritage Foundation, 2011), 7.

2. Ibid., 3–7.

3. Irving Kristol, *The Neoconservative Persuasion: Selected Essays,*
1942–2009 (New York: Basic Books, 2011), 306.

4. Matthew Spalding, *The Founders' Almanac* (Washington, DC:
Heritage Foundation, 2002), 191.

5. Eisenhower's remarks were cited by Bill Federer on his daily
radio show, *American Minute,* February 3, 2011.

6. United States Commission on International Religious
Freedom, http://www.uscirf.gov/images/annual%20report%20
2010.pdf.

7. George Washington, Farewell Address, September 19, 1796,
cited in Spalding, *Founders' Almanac,* 192.

8. Matthew Spalding, *We Still Hold These Truths: Rediscovering Our
Principles, Reclaiming Our Future* (Wilmington, DE: ISI Books,
2010), 63.

9. Ryan Messmore, "Government for the Good of the People:
Ten Questions About Freedom, Virtue, and the Role of
Government," Heritage *WebMemo* no. 1620, September 17, 2007.

10. Cited in Spalding, *We Still Hold These Truths,* 61.

Chapter 11: The Law

1. Edwin Meese, in Paul Rosenzweig and Brian W. Walsh, *One
Nation Under Arrest: How Crazy Laws, Rogue Prosecutors, and
Activist Judges Threaten Your Liberty* (Washington, DC: Heritage
Foundation, 2010), xviii.

2. Abner Schoenwetter, *Testimony before Subcommittee on Crime,
Terrorism, and Homeland Security,* Committee on the Judiciary,
United States House of Representatives, September 28, 2010.

3. Gary Fields and John R. Emshwiller, "As Criminal Laws
Proliferate, More Are Ensnared," *Wall Street Journal,* July 23,
2011.

4. Rosenzweig and Walsh, *One Nation Under Arrest,* xx.

5. Cited in ibid., 226.

Chapter 12: Tolerance and Open-Mindedness

1. Leszek Kolakowski, *Freedom, Fame, Lying, and Betrayal* (Boulder,
CO: Westview Press, 1999), 39.

2. Robert H. Bork, *Slouching Towards Gomorrah: Modern Liberalism
and American Decline* (New York: Regan Books, 1996), 141.

3. Irving Kristol, *The Neoconservative Persuasion: Selected Essays 1942–2009* (New York: Basic Books, 2011), 310.
4. Bork, *Slouching Towards Gomorrah*, 148.
5. Ibid., 146.
6. Matthew Spalding, *We Still Hold These Truths: Rediscovering Our Principles, Reclaiming Our Future* (Wilmington, DE: ISI Books, 2010), 210.
7. Edwin J. Feulner Jr., "Presidential Address delivered to the 1998 General Meeting of the Mont Pelerin Society," quoted in *Intellectual Pilgrims: The Fiftieth Anniversary of the Mont Pelerin Society* (Washington, DC: Heritage Foundation, 1999), 50–51.
8. "So it's not surprising then that they get bitter, they cling to guns or religion or antipathy to people who aren't like them or anti-immigrant sentiment or anti-trade sentiment as a way to explain their frustrations." Senator Barack Obama, April 11, 2008.

Chapter 13: Idealistic Realism

1. Leszek Kolakowski, *Freedom, Fame, Lying and Betrayal* (Boulder, CO: Westview Press, 1999), 32.
2. Rachel Sheffield, "FamilyFacts.org: Education Spending Skyrockets While Achievement Remains Flat," posted on *Foundry*, March 9, 2011.
3. Robert L. Woodson Sr. cited in Jay Richards, *What Causes Poverty in America?* (Washington, DC: Heritage Foundation, 2010), 10.

Chapter 14: Pragmatism

1. Larry Schweikart and Michael Allen, *A Patriot's History of the United States* (New York: Penguin, 2004), 343.
2. James Gordon Bennett, cited on Thinkexist.com.
3. Thomas Paine, "The American Crisis I," *Collected Writings: Common Sense, the Crisis, and Other Pamphlets, Articles, and Letters ; Rights of Man ; The Age of Reason*, ed. Eric Foner (New York: Literary Classics of the United States, 1995), 91. (Paine's work originally published December 19, 1776.)
4. H. W. Crocker III, *Don't Tread on Me* (New York: Crown Forum, 2006), 59.
5. David Hackett Fischer, *Washington's Crossing* (New York: Oxford University Press, 2004), 365.

6. Cited in Lee Edwards, *A Brief History of the Modern American Conservative Movement* (Washington, DC: Heritage Foundation, 2004), 16.
7. Lee Edwards, *William F. Buckley Jr.: The Maker of a Movement* (Wilmington, DE: ISI Books, 2010), 189.
8. Ibid., 136–37.
9. Ibid., 191.
10. http://www.briantracy.com/blog/personal-success/using-stumbling-blocks-as-stepping-stones/.
11. Milton Friedman, cited in Edward J. Feulner Jr., *The March of Freedom: Modern Classics in Conservative Thought* (Washington, DC: Heritage Books, 2003), 116.
12. Bruce Bawer, "The Closing of the Liberal Mind," in Adam Bellow, *New Threats to Freedom* (West Conshohocken, PA: Templeton Press, 2010), 22.

Chapter 15: Problem Solving

1. Address by Benjamin Franklin at the Federal Convention on September 17, 1787, as recorded in James Madison's notes on the Convention. From: *The Records of the Federal Convention of 1787*, Vol. II, Max Farrand ed., (Newhaven and London: Yale University Press, 1966), 641–42.
2. Alexis de Tocqueville, "What Kind of Despotism Democratic Nations Have to Fear," in *Democracy in America*, vol. 2 (1840), quoted in Matthew Spalding, *We Still Hold These Truths: Rediscovering Our Principles, Reclaiming Our Future* (Wilmington, DE: ISI Books, 2010), 218.
3. Cited in Irving Kristol, *The Neoconservative Persuasion: Selected Essays, 1942–2009* (New York: Basic Books, 2011), 97.
4. Jonah Goldberg, *Liberal Fascism: The Secret History of the American Left from Mussolini to the Politics of Meaning* (New York: Doubleday, 2008), 393.
5. Kristol, *The Neoconservative Persuasion*, 96.

Chapter 16: Generosity

1. George Washington, Letter to Bushrod Washington, Newburgh, January 15, 1783.
2. Indiana University Center for Philanthropy, http://www.philanthropy.iupui.edu/Research/Giving/Hurricane_Katrina.aspx.

3. Congressional Research Service, http://www.au.af.mil/au/awc/awcgate/crs/rs22239.pdf.
4. Philanthropy News Digest, http://foundationcenter.org/pnd/news/story.jhtml?id=165300011.
5. $1.3 billion, citing CNN here, http://money.cnn.com/2010/07/09/news/international/haiti_donation/index.htm.
6. Philanthropy News Digest, http://foundationcenter.org/pnd/news/story.jhtml?id=165300011.
7. USAID.gov, http://www.usaid.gov/rdma/articles/press_release_600.html.
8. Cited in *Poor Richard's Almanack*, http://www.unsv.com/voanews/specialenglish/scripts/2010/11/07/0040/Poor_Richard's_Almanack_by_Franklin_Benjamin.pdf
9. Ryan Messmore, "Charitable Giving Benefits Giver as Much as Receiver," Heritage *Commentary*, December 23, 2006.
10. Ryan Messmore, "Obama's Latest Proposal to Reduce Charitable Deductions Would Crowd Out Civil Society," Heritage *Backgrounder* no. 2538, March 29, 2011.

Chapter 17: Capitalism

1. Steve Forbes, "Enterprise," in Edwin J. Feulner Jr., *Leadership for America: The Principles of Conservatism* (Dallas: Spence Publishing Company, 2000), 131.
2. Ibid., 134.
3. Kim R. Holmes and Matthew Spalding, *Understanding America: Why Does Economic Freedom Matter?* (Washington, DC: Heritage Foundation, 2011), 13.
4. Edwin J. Feulner Jr., *The March of Freedom: Modern Classics in Conservative Thought* (Washington, DC: Heritage Foundation, 2002), xxi.
5. Brian Tracy, *Victory!* (New York: AMACOM, 2002), 42.
6. Cited in Lee Edwards, *A Brief History of the Modern American Conservative Movement* (Washington, DC: Heritage Foundation, 2004), 67.
7. From "Rich States, Poor States," Art Laffer, Steve Moore, and Jonathan Williams, http://www.alec.org/AM/Template.cfm?Section=Rich_States_Poor_States.
8. Michael C. Moynihan, "The Anticapitalists," in Adam Bellow, *New Threats to Freedom* (West Conshohocken, PA: Templeton Press, 2010), 191.

9. Milton and Rose Friedman, *Free to Choose: A Personal Statement* (New York: Mariner Books, 1990), quoted in Edwin J. Feulner Jr., *Intellectual Pilgrims: The Fiftieth Anniversary of the Mont Pelerin Society* (Washington, DC: Heritage Foundation, 1999), 34.

10. Kenneth Minogue, cited in Edwin J. Feulner Jr., "Remarks to Mont Pelerin Society" (Buenos Aires, Argentina, April 17, 2011).

Chapter 18: Education

1. "Approximately 1.5 million children (2.9 percent of school-age children) were being homeschooled in the spring of 2007, representing a 36 percent relative increase since 2003 and a 74 percent relative increase since 1999. One private researcher estimates that as many as 2.5 million school-age children were educated at home during the 2007–2008 school year." See Lindsey Burke, "Homeschooling Sees Dramatic Rise in Popularity," Heritage *WebMemo*, January 28, 2009.

2. Lindsey Burke, "Creating a Crisis: Unions Stifle Education Reform," Heritage *WebMemo* no. 2967, July 20, 2010. More generally, apart from political parties, government-employee unions spend more than other groups on US elections. See James Sherk, "Time to Restore Voter Control: End the Government-Union Monopoly," Heritage *Backgrounder* no. 2522, February 25, 2011.

3. Lindsey Burke, "The Unabashed Dismantling of the DC Opportunity Scholarship Program," Heritage *Commentary*, February 23, 2010.

4. The White House, cited in "SOAR Act Throws Kids an Educational Lifeline," *Foundry*, March 31, 2011.

5. Tiffany Dunston, Congressional Hearing on the D.C. Opportunity Scholarship Program, United States Senate Committee on Homeland Security and Governmental Affairs, May 13, 2009.

Chapter 19: Money and Taxes

1. Denise Kersten Wills, "Sweet Taste of Success," *Philanthropy Magazine*, Fall 2009.

2. Abraham Lincoln, speech at New Haven, Connecticut, March 6, 1860, quoted in Peter Wehner and Arthur C. Brooks, *Wealth*

and Justice: The Morality of Democratic Capitalism (Washington, DC: AEI Press, 2011), 55–56.

3. 1 Tim. 6:10 KJV

4. Gen. 13:2 KJV

5. Matt. 25:21 ESV

6. Matt. 25:26 ESV

7. Marvin Olasky, "Profit: Prophets and Profit," in *Indivisible: Social and Economic Foundations of American Liberty* (Washington, DC: Heritage Foundation, 2010), 39, 41.

8. Curtis S. Dubay, "Income Tax Will Become More Progressive Under Obama Tax Plan," Heritage *Backgrounder* no. 2280, June 1, 2009.

9. Adam Smith, *An Inquiry into the Nature and Causes of the Wealth of Nations*, book 10, chapter 2.

10. Robert H. Bork, *Slouching Towards Gomorrah: Modern Liberalism and American Decline* (New York: Regan Books, 1996), 74.

11. "What Makes the Economy Grow?" Vol. 1 in a series from the Heritage Foundation, 13–15.

12. Rudy Giuliani, foreword to Steve Forbes and John Prevas, *Power Ambition Glory* (New York: Crown Business, 2009), x.

13. Dubay, "Income Tax Will Become More Progressive."

14. James Gattuso, "Red Tape Rises Again," *Foundry*, September 22, 2010.

15. Diane Katz, "Rolling Back Red Tape: Twenty Regulations to Eliminate," Heritage *Backgrounder* no. 2510, January 26, 2011.

Chapter 20: Courage

1. Stephen Crane, "The Veteran," in Amy A. Kass, Leon R. Kass, and Diana Schaub, *What So Proudly We Hail: The American Soul in Story, Speech and Song* (Wilmington, DE: ISI Books, 2011), 331.

2. www.military-quotes.com/churchill.htm.

3. Peggy Noonan, *When Character Was King* (New York: Penguin Books Ltd, 2002), 279.

4. Elizabeth Downey, "A Fitting Tribute to a Slain Navy SEAL Gains Attention," FOXNews.com, July 4, 2008.

5. www.great-quotes.com/quote/334.

6. Edwin Meese, "The Leadership Lessons of Ronald Reagan," in *Leadership Letters: A Publication of the Ronald W. Reagan Leadership Program at Eureka College*, Fall/Winter 2010, 7.

7. Margaret Thatcher, "Courage," in Edwin J. Feulner Jr., *Leadership for America: The Principles of Conservatism* (Dallas: Spence Publishing Company, 2000), 7.

8. Heritage scholars have published a detailed plan to get America's fiscal house in order by balancing the budget within a decade, reducing the debt, and cutting government in half. See Stuart Butler, Alison Acosta Fraser, and William Beach, *Saving the American Dream: The Heritage Plan to Fix the Debt, Cut Spending, and Restore Prosperity*, Heritage Special Report no. 91, May 10, 2011.

9. Patrick Henry, cited in Matthew Spalding, *The Founders' Almanac* (Washington, DC: Heritage Foundation, 2002), 143.

10. Oliver Wendell Holmes Jr., "In Our Youth Our Hearts Were Touched with Fire," cited in Kass, Kass, and Schaub, *What So Proudly We Hail*, 697.

11. Cited in Ronald Reagan, *Speaking My Mind: Selected Speeches* (New York: Simon & Schuster, 1989), 140–42. President Reagan also cited this letter in his January 11, 1989, Farewell Address to the Nation.

About the Authors

Edwin J. Feulner, Ph.D., is the president of the Heritage Foundation, Washington's leading public policy think tank. Dr. Feulner has studied at the University of Edinburgh, the London School of Economics, the Wharton School of the University of Pennsylvania, and Regis University. He is also the author of six books, including *Getting America Right*.

Brian Tracy is chairman and CEO of Brian Tracy International, a company specializing in the training and development of organizations and individuals. Tracy has studied, researched, written, and spoken for thirty years in the fields of economics, history, and business. He has authored more than forty-five books.

Index